ONE CHURCH

WHAT WOULD IT BE LIKE?

ROBERT WYETH

WORKBOOK PRESS LLC
187 E Warm Springs Rd,
Suite B285, Las Vegas, NV 89119, USA

Website: https://workbookpress.com/
Hotline: 1-888-818-4856
Email: admin@workbookpress.com

Ordering Information:
Quantity sales. Special discounts are available on quantity purchases by corporations, associations, and others.
For details, contact the publisher at the address above.

Library of Congress Control Number:
ISBN-13:   978-1-958176-46-7 (Paperback Version)
                978-1-958176-47-4 (Digital Version)

REV. DATE: 05/24/2022

One Church What Would It Be Like?

Robert Wyeth

CONTENTS

ACKNOWLEDGEMENTS

Most of the verses were taken from the NIV Bible:

The Holy Bible, New International Version ®, copyright 1973, 1978, 1984 by International Bible Society.

Copyright 1985 by the Zondervan Corporation.

Anglicisation 1987 by the Hodder and Stoughton Limited.

This edition first presented in Great Britain in 1987.

Other versions:

Holy Bible, New Living Translation ®, copyright © 1996, 2004 by Tyndale Charitable Trust, issued by the Tyndale House Publishers.

The Holy Bible containing the Old and New Testaments the New King James Version. Copyright © 1979, 1980 by Thomas Nelson Inc. Published by Broadman & Holman Publishers, Nashville. Tennessee.

It contains the 1611 version of the Authorised Version for the Holy Scriptures.

SUMMARY

At the end of his life on earth when he was being taken up by God. A cloud hid Jesus from the disciples' sight. Before he went Jesus said,

"All authority in heaven and on earth has been given to me. Therefore, go and make disciples of all nations, baptising them in the name of the Father and of the Son and of the Holy Spirit, and teaching them to obey everything I have commanded you." Matthew ch.28 v18-20

However, the church did not do what Jesus instructed them. They copied something of what he told them, but they followed the traditions of their elders and leaders.

Consider the book of Nehemiah. He was authorised to go to Jerusalem to rebuild the wall (ch.2 v6), but the non-Jews heard about it they were furious (ch.2 v19; ch.4 v7). Finally, the wall was finished (ch.6 v15) and the Jews fasted, wearing sackcloth and having dust on their heads (ch.9 v1).

Then Nehemiah went back to his master (ch.13 v6). The people returned to what they had been doing, back to their traditions:

A non-Jew took over a room in the temple (ch.13 v7).

The provisions for the Levites had not been carried out (ch.13 v10).

The Sabbath was not kept (ch.13 v15).

Men were coming into Jerusalem on the Sabbath (ch.13 v16).

People were married off to the Gentiles (ch.13 v23).

In Nehemiah, you start with what is good, but the false teachers and false prophets came in and convinced the Israelites to amend their ways. Amazing! even after completing the wall, still the Israelites returned to their traditions. When Nehemiah left to go back to king Artaxerxes over 800 miles away.

Peter said,

"But there were also false prophets among the people, just as there will be false teachers among you. They will secretly introduce destructive heresies, even denying the sovereign Lord who bought them - bringing swift destruction on themselves. Many will follow their shameful ways and will bring the way of truth into disrepute" 2 Peter ch.2 v1-2

We can follow the believers at the end of the first century. It is all laid down for us to see how they managed to recover from the sins of the past and what they were currently doing.

THE EARLY CHURCH

THE CHURCH IS ONE BODY

Jesus prays for all believers before he was arrested and taken by the Jews and handed over to the Romans to be executed (see John ch.17 v2-26).

He understood that this was his last hour before he was crucified. He was going back to the Father. Before he went he spoke to his Father:

He prays for himself.

He prays for his disciples.

He prays for all the believers.

Jesus says, *"I have given them the glory that you gave me, that they may be one as we are one: I in them and you in me. May they be brought to complete unity to let the world know that you sent me and have loved them even as you have loved me."* John ch.17 v22-23

Unity: He prayed for that unity that is harmony, solidarity and oneness. It is not disunity, disagreement and discord. Not to separate off, but have complete agreement and that the church would be strong and vibrant.

For the rest of the Bible, the church fought together as one. There were a series of false teachers and prophets in the church. But they stayed together, as one, they remained as one throughout the Bible.

However, it is not unity that binds them together, it is more than that.

JESUS ASKED THEM TO GO

Jesus had told them what to do: 'Go and make disciples of all nations, baptising them in the name of God. Teaching them to obey everything that I have commanded you' (see Matthew ch.28 v18-20).

Most people do not enter the church except when they are married, baptise children and die. It is a comfortable, safe place to go to church where you might be protected and have the outside world passing by. You could easily spend some there, looking at the furnishings, pillars, windows, seats and hear the readings and prayers from the Bible.

However, Jesus said, 'Go'. It is a call for all the nations, to go outside. It was a reminder for us today, to get out and teach and preach what God says in the Bible.

Baptism is an important step to witness outside where many people could be staying and watching. It is a crucial step to belong to the believers. To count the cost of being prepared to do that. It is a reminder of Jesus being killed, buried and raised again as you come out of the water.

Teaching them what Jesus has commanded. To shepherd them and keep them true to the faith. If you don't do it, people would depart from the truth being convinced by what many others believe. There are a lot of false prophets and teachers in the church and we have it today. It is impossible to remove them. This is why the apostles wrote letters to the churches to remind them to follow the truth.

Jesus would be there to lead the believers up until the end of the age. This is certainly true, the church will follow his guidance and the Bible is the way to practise what he has commanded.

JESUS WAS GLORIFIED

When Jesus was taken up before their very eyes and a cloud hid him from their view. They were looking up to see if he might come back. But two angels appeared and explained to them, 'Why were they standing there looking'. They returned to Jerusalem to carry on with the work without Jesus.

What things did the disciples do:

> Feeding the poor?

> Going to the Temple?

> Explaining to the Sadducees?

> Teaching the people?

> Witnessing?

But they didn't do even that. They waited for the coming of the Spirit of God to enable them to go.

A Sabbath's day's walk from the city. When they arrived they went upstairs to the room where they had been staying ... Therefore, it is necessary to choose one of the men who have been with us the whole time the Lord Jesus went in and out among us. Acts ch.1 v12-13, v21

It is significant that they addressed what would happen to Judas Iscariot who betrayed Jesus. To make up for another apostle who had been with Jesus, he knew what Jesus wanted and for the work still to be done.

They chose Matthias, so he was added to the eleven apostles (see Acts ch.1 v26), but the scripture is silent about what he did as an apostle.

Feast of Pentecost

When the Holy Spirit came upon them at the Feast of Pentecost. They were filled with the Holy Spirit and then they went out in Jerusalem to teach and preach.

Suddenly a sound like the blowing of a violent wind came from heaven and filled the whole house where they were sitting. They saw what seemed like tongues of fire that separated and came to rest on each of them. All of them were filled with the Holy Spirit and began to speak in other tongues as the Spirit enabled them. Acts ch.2 v2-4

The Holy Spirit came on them to equip them. If they didn't have the Holy Spirit, nothing would be done. All of them were chosen to go and do what Jesus had commanded.

It started with Jerusalem where they were staying, but branched out under a great persecution against the church at Jerusalem. For the word would go to the whole of the Roman Empire including Jews and Gentiles.

This work is still with us, we must go and tell the rest of the world that Jesus died, was buried and rose again. A Saviour and Lord, not buried in the church buildings, but nobody goes there apart from a few Christians.

Fellowship of Believers

Every day they met together in the temple courts praising God. Because they didn't have the chance to build places where they could meet. Th e Lord added to their number those who were being saved. But it was outside not in a church.

They devoted themselves to the apostles' teaching and to the fellowship, to the breaking of bread and to prayer. Everyone was filled with awe, and many wonders and miraculous signs were done by the apostles. All the believers were together and had everything in common. Acts ch.2 v42-44

What did they do?

Apostles teaching.

Fellowship.

Breaking of bread in their homes (see Acts ch.2 v46).

Prayer.

This was the early work to guide the apostles' teaching to the believers in what they should say to the rest of the world.

When Jesus after he was crucified and rose again he said to Simon Peter (see John ch.21 v15-17), 'Do you love me?' Take care of all of my sheep:

Feed my lambs.

Take care of my sheep.

Feed my sheep.

This was when Jesus was not around, Peter (an apostle) will have to take care of 'shepherding his sheep'. This is why the apostles' teaching was so important to give the believers something to hold on to. Much later, when the missionary journeys were going on, the believers were all of different places and so Paul said that they would have 'elders' at each place to guide the believers.

The apostles were only twelve but the elders had many churches all around in the Roman world. Syria, Asia Minor, Greece and so on. The elders were responsible for guiding and leading the church. This is why the elders should be respected and honoured.

Everyone was filled with awe at what the apostles did with miraculous signs and wonders. They sold their possessions and goods and they gave to anyone who had need of them. It was basically faith and deeds (see James ch.2 v14-26).

Like Paul who spoke before king Agrippa:

"I preached that they should repent and turn to God and prove their repentance by their deeds." Acts ch.26 v20

It was faith first, and then the poor by their deeds.

PETER AND JOHN BEFORE THE SANHEDRIN

The priests and the captain of the temple guard and the Sadducees came up to Peter and John while they were speaking to the people. They were greatly disturbed because the apostles were teaching the people and proclaiming in Jesus the resurrection of the dead. Acts ch.4 v1-2

When they saw the courage of Peter and John and realised that they were unschooled, ordinary men, they were astonished and they took note that these men had been with Jesus. Acts ch.4 v13

The Sanhedrin realised that Peter and John were teaching the people, not hidden away with the door shut tight against the Jews. They knew that these men had been with Jesus. They were deeply troubled and confounded. They didn't realise the Holy Spirit had come upon them and changed them.

They were unschooled, ordinary men. They didn't have the privilege of being part of the Sanhedrin, they couldn't have known all the Torah (the known law of the Jews) that had been passed down for generations, they couldn't know about the prophets and the kings because they were simply fishermen.

They were casting a net into the lake, for they were fishermen ... They were in the boat with their father Zebedee preparing their nets. Matthew ch.4 v18, v21

They did what their father Zebedee did, to make a living catching fish. They had boats and nets which their father presumably owned.

They saw the man who had been healed was a beggar who was sitting in Solomon's Colonnade before all the people. This was the fact that they had seen and witnessed, the resurrection of Jesus from the dead. They had understood and observed, that's why the people believed. The church grew to about five thousand men.

But thy could see the man who had been silent, standing there. He was able to walk again, not with sticks. His feet and ankles grew strong again so it was a miracle that Peter and John had achieved. No wonder the crowd was ecstatic and cheerful. God would come to rescue them and the church was something to be proud of.

The Sanhedrin could not decide how to punish the men because all the people were praising God for what had happened. The man who was healed, he was forty years old and he had been like that for years, nobody was interested in him, even the Sanhedrin.

Persecution in Jerusalem

In those days when the number of disciples was increasing, the Grecian Jews among them complained against the Hebraic Jews because their widows were being overlooked in the daily distribution of food. Acts ch.6 v1

The apostles gathered all the believers together and said,

"It is not right that we should neglect the ministry of the word in order to wait on tables." Acts ch.6 v2

Choose seven men among you who are known to be full of the Spirit and wisdom and we will let them worry about this matter. They choose Stephen, a man full of God's grace and power.

Stephen, a man full of God's grace and power, did great wonders and miraculous signs among the people. Opposition arose, however from members of the Synagogue ... These men began to argue with Stephen, but they could not stand up against his wisdom or the Spirit by whom he spoke. Acts ch.6 v8-10

So they stirred up the people and elders of the teachers of the law. They seized Stephen and brought him before the Sanhedrin. In Acts ch.7, Stephen explained what he did and then he said,

"You stiff-necked people, with uncircumcised hearts and ears! You are just like your fathers: You always resist the Holy Spirit! Was there ever a prophet your fathers did not persecute? They even killed those who predicted the coming of the Righteous One. And now you have betrayed and murdered him." Acts ch.7 v51-52

They dragged Stephen out of the city, began to stone him and he died.

On that day a great persecution broke out against the church in Jerusalem, and all except the apostles were scattered throughout Judea and Samaria. Acts ch.8 v1

Before we come to the churches that were formed after that, first we must think about Jesus teaching his disciples or the church.

JESUS TEACHING THE CHURCH

After the temptation of Jesus, Satan was worried out him so he went out and began to preach and Jesus childhood was over.

Repent, for the kingdom of heaven is near." Matthew ch.4 v17

Jesus went through Galilee teaching in their synagogues, preaching the good new of the kingdom, and healing every disease and sickness among the people. News about him spread all over the Palestine.

When he saw the crowds he went up on a mountainside and he began to teach them in the book of Matthew, saying:

The Beatitudes	ch.5 v3-12
Salt and light	ch.5 v13-16
The fulfilment of the law	ch.5 v17-20
Murder	ch.5 v21-26
Adultery	ch.5 v27-30
Divorce	ch.5 v31-32
Oaths	ch.5 v33-37

An eye for an eye	ch.5 v38-42
Love for enemies	ch.5 v43-48
Giving to the needy	ch.6 v1-4
Prayer	ch.6 v5-15
Fasting	ch.6 v16-18
Treasures in heaven	ch.6 v19-24
Do not worry	ch.6 v25-34
Judging others	ch.7 v1-6
Ask, seek, knock	ch.7 v7-12
Narrow and wide gates	ch.7 v13-14
A tree and its fruit	ch.7 v15-23
Wise and foolish builders	ch.7 v24-27

This is not the whole sum of what Jesus taught, but it is a good starting place. It is a call to moral and ethical thinking, there is no doubt that Jesus gave the sermon as a standard for all believers, realising that its demands cannot be met in our own power. This relies on the Holy Spirit living in us.

The Beatitudes: When we work and think, blessed are those who reflect on Jesus love and they will receive help from above.

Salt and light: We are the salt and light of the world. If we lose the saltiness or hide the light, it is not good. Let you light shine before men that they may see what works that you do.

The fulfilment of the law: Jesus has not come to abolish the law but to fulfil the law. Anyone who breaks the law will be called least in the kingdom of heaven.

Murder: Anyone who is angry with his brother is capable of murder. First go and be reconciled to your brother. Settle matters quickly with your adversary.

Adultery: Anyone who looks at a woman lustfully has already committed adultery with her. It will be better to lose one part of your body to avoid the hell to which you are going.

Divorce: A man who divorces his wife except for marital unfaithfulness. Anyone who marries a divorced woman commits adultery.

Oaths: Do not swear at all. This comes by the evil one from Satan.

An eye for an eye: Do not resist an evil person. Give to the one who wants to borrow something from you.

Love for enemies: Love your enemies and pray for those who persecute you. God causes his sun to rise on the evil and the good.

Giving to the needy: When you give to the needy do not announce it. Then your Father who sees what you do will reward you.

Prayer: When you pray, go into your room, close the door and pray to your Father. Let your words be short, for your Father knows what you need before you ask him. Forgive men for their sins.

Fasting: When you fast, hide it and it will not be obvious to men that you are fasting.

Treasures in heaven: Do not store up for yourselves treasures on earth, but store up treasures in heaven. You cannot serve both God and money.

Do not worry: Do not worry about your life. Your heavenly Father knows that you need them. Each day has enough trouble of its own.

Judging others: Do not judge, or you too will be judged. With the measure you use, it will be measured to you.

Ask, seek, knock: For everyone who ask receives, he who seeks finds and to him who knocks the door will be opened. Your Father in heaven will give good gifts to those who ask him.

The narrow and wide gates: For wide is the gate that lead to destruction but small is the gate that leads to life and only a few find it.

A tree and its fruit: Watch out for false prophets. Likewise, every good tree bears good fruit, but a bad tree bears bad fruit.

The wise and foolish builders: Everyone who hears these words of mine and puts them into practice and does them.

When Jesus had finished saying these things, the crowds were amazed at his teaching, because he taught at one who had authority, and not as their teachers of the law. Matthew ch.7 v28-29

It is the Spirit of God who dwells in a believer and that makes all the difference.

You, however, are controlled not by the sinful nature but by the Spirit, if the Spirit of God lives in you. Romans ch.8 v9

THE WORD CHURCH

Church in the Greek means 'ekklesia' and it is one single word. If it is churches, it would be 'ekklesias', which mostly means a local congregation and never a building. They didn't have the expertise or money to construct a dwelling to meet together.

Although we often speak of these congregations collectively as the New Testament Church or the Early Church, no New Testament writer uses 'ekklesia' in this way. An 'ekklesia' was a meeting or assembly rather than an organisation or society.

Locality, was essential to its character. While there might be as many as local churches as there were cities, or even households, yet the New Testament only recognises one 'ekklesia' without finding it necessary to explain the rest of the others churches.

The church was a heavenly reality, a real-world existence.

God placed all things under his feet and appointed him to be head over everything for the church, which is his body, the fullness of him who fills everything in every way. Ephesians ch.1 v22

Yet since the local 'ekklesia' was gathered together in Christ's name and had him in its midst, it tasted the powers of the age to come.

Jesus said, "For where two of three come together in my name, there am I with them." Matthew ch.18 v20

It was critical to let the apostles explain the teaching of Jesus and certain elders who could 'shepherd the sheep' to let them grow in the faith.

Keep watch over yourselves and all the flock of which the Holy Spirit has made you overseers. Be shepherds of the church of God, which he bought with his own blood. Acts ch.20 v28

The church was a meeting in a place, not a society which we unfortunately had today. Like Anglican, Baptist, Brethren, Methodist and so on, it is a club which all the other members outside are not very welcome. Whether they are believers.

THE WORD LOVE

We all have different situations in life and many versions of the Bible, so why are there clashes and opposition to the Scriptures?

Now you are the body of Christ, and each one of you is a part of it. 1 Corinthians ch.12 v27

Each one is useful, to make up the body. Don't think that you are not part of his realm, not being useful, not preaching or teaching, not keeping the church clean. Illness keeps you away from doing most things and your handicap means that you are in a wheelchair. But your inner glow makes you special and the Spirit of God keeps you alive.

God is kind to the ungrateful and wicked.

Be merciful, just as your Father is merciful. Luke ch.6 v36

God doesn't send the sun and the rain on the righteous but he allows it for the good and the bad. God is merciful and you must be loving and caring. Even in the church where there is some disagreement. This is where the elders looking to Jesus teaching, come to point out the truths that we should all follow.

May they be brought to complete unity to let the world know that you sent me and have loved them even as you have loved me. John ch.17 v23

Jesus' prayer is a rebuke of the groundless and often bitter divisions among Christians. He believed that everybody would be one. Not a lot of churches all participating in worship, scripture and deeds. Not really holding out their hands towards others who do the same.

God does not judge by external appearance ... The only things that counts is faith expressing itself through love. Galatians ch.2 v6; ch.5 v6

The Lord doesn't judge by the works we do, but he looks at the heart. The soul and mind. What does he see? You can hide most things, but you can't hide love.

Jesus was going to Jerusalem, he was worried about the cross he had to bear for the sins of the world. But he stopped on the way. He let the children come to him and he loved them. This is the heart of a good man.

When he had placed his hands on them (the children), he went on from there. Matthew ch.19 v15

The word 'love' means that the heart of man in the church must shine out. Be ready to forgive others who fail to do what Jesus taught. We can see in the church there will be false prophets and false teachers who lead the church away. This is what the apostles considered so important that they wrote several letters including Romans, 2 Corinthians, Colossians,

Hebrews, 1 and 2 Peter. John's Epistles and Jude (all in Biblical order).

Love is patient, love is kind. It does not envy, it does not boast, it is not proud. It is not rude, it is not self-seeking, it is not easily angered, it keeps no record of wrongs. Love does not delight in evil but rejoice with the truth. It always protects, always trusts, always hopes, always perseveres. Love never fails. 1 Corinthians ch.13 v4-8

But if the elders are not willing to carry the words and teaching of Jesus, he will remove the church from his body. The church will be there carrying on, worshipping, singing but the Holy Spirit would not be there. It will be dead.

Like the some of the churches in the book of Revelation:

Ephesus - *I will come to you and remove your lampstand from its place. Revelation ch.2 v5*

Pergamum - *I will soon come to you and will fight against them. Revelation ch.2 v16*

Thyatira - *I will strike her children dead. Revelation ch.2 v23*

Sardis - *I will come like a thief, and you will not know at what time I will come to you. Revelation ch.3 v3*

Laodicea - *I am about to spit you out of my mouth. Revelation ch.3 v16*

Five out of seven churches all had problems and if they don't repent God would remove the churches. This is why there are difficulties with the false prophets and false teachers in the church. This is not a good sign, even when the New Testament was written. Even the apostles in their letters to the churches reminded of them of troubling concern that Jesus taught on this earth. The elders should and must 'shepherd the sheep'.

Brother Who Sins Against You

Any brother who sins against you go round and explain what he has done, to explain what will happen to him.

Jesus said, "If your brother sins against you, go and show him his fault, just between the two of you. If he listens to you, you have won your brother over. But if he will not listen, take one of two others along, so that 'every matter may be established by the testimony of two of three witnesses.' " Matthew ch.18 v15-16

It is important that you forgive each other. Not, seven times but all of the time!

Then Peter came to Jesus and asked, "Lord, how many times shall I forgive my brother when he sins against me? Up to seven times?" Jesus answered, "I tell you, not seven times, but seventy-seven times." Matthew ch.18 v21-22

When Jesus taught the disciples to pray (see Matthew ch.6 v9-15), he said:

Our Father in heaven.

Holy be your name.

Your kingdom come.

Your will be done.

Give us today our daily food.

Forgive us our sins.

We also have forgiven others.

Lead us not into temptation.

Deliver us from the evil one.

It is important that you forgive others while you are telling God how sorry you are and confessing your sins. Jesus reminded the disciples of the parable of the unmerciful servant (see Matthew ch.18 v23-35).

"You wicked servant," he said, "I cancelled that debt of yours because you begged me to. Shouldn't you have had mercy on your fellow-servant just as I had on you?" Matthew ch.18 v32-33

"This is how my heavenly Father will treat each of you unless you forgive your brother from your heart." Mathew ch.18 v35

God will expect you to forgive each other. Not once, but many times.

The Bishop of Rome

We know that Clement of Rome (AD 35-89) is noted as the first Roman Bishop. After Paul and Peter were killed by the Emperor Nero, Clement was with the Jerusalem church and became the leader of the church there.

There was a dispute within the church at Corinth, with a split by the election of a new group of leaders and the enforced resignation of their predecessors. Clement wrote a long letter to the church. He was in Rome at the time and he is known as Pope Clement I. He was imprisoned by order of Emperor Trajan and thereafter being executed by being tied to an anchor and thrown into the sea.

They had elders and deacons to manage the church but not a bishop to oversee what was going on for so many churches.

In Paul's letter to Timothy and Titus he had sure that an elder must be a man whose life is above reproach, and deacons must be men and well respected and have integrity (see 1 Timothy ch.3 v1-13; ch.5 v17 and Titus ch.1 v6-9).

Peter reminds the elders among you:

Be shepherds of God's flock that is under your care, serving as oversees - not because you must, but because you are willing, as God's wants you to be. 1

Peter ch.5 v2

The bishop is a deviation from what Jesus had taught and instructed.

Paul and Timothy, servants of Christ Jesus. To all the saints in Christ Jesus at Philippi, together with the overseers and deacons. Philippians ch.1 v1

There are only two local church officers mentioned in the New Testament are those of overseers (also called elders) and the deacons.

EXCOMMUNICATION FROM THE CHURCH

The church is one, what about those who are excluded from the church?

Some wandered in desert wastelands, find no way to a city where they could settle. They were hungry and thirsty, and their lives ebbed away. Psalm ch.107 v4-5

They were Israelites wandering around in the desert.

Remember at that time you were separate from Christ ... without hope and without God in the world. Ephesians ch.2 v12

These expressions emphasise the distance of unbelieving Gentiles from Israel, as well as from Christ.

In the Parable of the Sower (see Matthew ch.13 v1-23), Jesus explains what the sower meant when he sowed the seeds.

"The one who received the seed that fell on rocky places is the man who hears the word and at once receives it with joy. But since he had no root, he lasts only a short time. When trouble or persecution comes because of the word, he quickly falls away." Matthew ch.13 v20-21

The man hears the word and at once receives it gladly. He didn't really have understanding, it is a short while he was in the church. Trouble or persecution arises and he quickly falls away. Why did he not have understanding? Because he didn't have the Spirit of God to instruct or help him.

Those who live in accordance with the Spirit have their minds set on what the Spirit desires ... If anyone does not have the Spirit of Christ, he does not belong to Christ. Romans ch.8 v5, v9

If you hear the God's word speaking to you, male or female who rejects the word of God knowing too well the value of coming to faith. Who spurns the Holy Spirit and ignores him? If they fall way God will not hold out his hand for them. They are on their own.

It is impossible for those who have once been enlightened, who have tasted the heavenly gift, who have shared in the Holy Spirit, who have tasted the goodness of the word of God, and the powers of the coming age, if they fall away, to be brought back to repentance, because to their loss they are crucifying the Son of God all over again and subjecting him to public disgrace. Hebrews ch.6 v4-6

If they adamantly turned away from God against the light they had received, proving they never have been regenerated.

It would have been better for them not to have known the way of righteousness, than to have known it and then to turn their backs on the sacred command that was passed on to them. 2 Peter ch.2 v21

Jesus is calling to you, 'Repent, to change your mind and attitude'. He is calling on you to repent and believe.

Remember the height from which you have fallen! Repent! and do the things you did at first. If you do not repent, I will come to you and remove your lampstand from its place. Revelation ch.2 v5

Remember the height you first had. Repent and do the important things, or I will surely come to you. It will be an immediate judgement. God is not mocked or ridiculed or insulted.

The unbelieving ... their place will be their fiery lake of burning sulphur. This is the second death. Revelation ch.22 v8

It is fearsome and tragic that those who reject the words of God, who spurn the Holy Spirit, who trample on what Jesus had done - these eventually will be thrown into the fire, and nobody could help them.

THE PRAYER OF FAITH

If any one of you in trouble? He should pray ... He should call on the elders of the church to pray over him and anoint him with oil in the name of the Lord. James ch.5 v13-14

The reason is not to exclude him, letting him go. But bring him back into the faith. This is the job of the elders, to 'shepherd the sheep'.

My brothers, if one of you should wander from the truth and someone should bring him back, remember this: Whoever turns a sinner from the error of his ways will save him from death and cover over a multitude of sins. James ch.5 v19-20

The purpose of the church is to be kind to any person who falls away and bring him back into the church. Not let hm go off to find anther church with a different kind of teaching. The church is only one, so there's no difference between God and man. It is the same Jesus Christ and the Holy Spirit. They are not changing.

So, we have come to the place where the churches are formed. Consider them and what they are doing.

THEIR MISSIONARY JOURNEYS

When we come to the churches, it is important that you understand from the verses how many journeys the apostles made in the book of Acts. For example:

Philip's missionary journey (see Acts ch.8 v5-40).

Peter's missionary journey (see Acts ch.9 v32 - ch.12 v19).

Paul's (AD 46-48) first missionary journey with Barnabas (see Acts ch.13 v4 - ch.14 v28).

Barnabas missionary journey with Mark in Crete (see Acts ch.15 v39).

Paul's (AD 49-52) second missionary journey with Silas (see Acts ch.15 v40 - ch.18 v22).

Paul's (AD 53-57) third missionary journey but he was on his own (see Acts ch.18 v23 - ch.21 v20).

Paul's (AD 59-60) forth missionary journey he was on his own as a prisoner (see Acts ch.27 v27 - ch.28 v16).

Paul's fifth missionary journey he went to Crete with him was Titus (see Acts ch.28 v17-31 and Titus ch.1 v1 - ch.3 v15).

Paul says, I have worked harder, been put in prison more often, been whipped times without number, and faced death again and again. Five different times the Jewish leaders gave me thirty-nine lashes. Three times I was beaten with rods. Once I was stoned. Three times I was shipwrecked. Once I spent a whole night and a day adrift at sea. I have travelled on many long journeys. I have faced danger from rivers and from robbers. I have faced danger from my own people, the Jews, as well as from the Gentiles. I have faced danger in the cities, in the deserts, and on the seas. And I have faced danger from men who claim to be believers but are not. I have worked hard and long, enduring many sleepless nights. I have been hungry and thirsty and have often gone without food. I have shivered in the cold, without enough clothing to keep me warm. Then, besides all this, I have the daily burden of my concern for all the churches. Who is weak without my feeling that weakness? Who is led astray, and I do not burn with anger? 2 Corinthians ch.11 v23-29

Paul went for over 15 years preaching and teaching the gospel and seeking all the believers to come into a church run by elders. As well as the persecution he suffered.

AROUND THE CHURCHES

PALESTINE

THE CHURCH IN CAESAREA

This magnificent city built by Herod the Great stood by the Mediterranean Sea. It was the Roman metropolis of Judea and the official residence of both the Herodian kings and the Roman procurators. There was a huge temple and an amphitheatre and many public buildings. Caesarea was also a trading centre for inland trade, it was based on the caravan route from Egypt to Tyre and it was also a trading centre for ships.

In the early stages of Stephen's persecution, Philip reached Caesarea.

Philip, however, appeared at Azotus and travelled about, preaching the gospel in all the towns until he reached Caesarea. Acts ch.8 v40

Paul was in Jerusalem before he went on to his missionary journeys. He met with Jesus on the Damascus road.

He talked and debated with the Grecian Jews, but they tried to kill him.

When the brothers learned of this, they took him down to Caesarea and sent him off to Tarsus. Acts ch.9 v29-30

.

The brothers sent him off to Tarsus of Cilicia where he was born (see Acts ch.22 v3).

At Caesarea there was a man named Cornelius, a centurion in what is known as the Italian Regiment. He and all his family were devout and God-fearing; he gave generously to those in need and prayed to God regularly. Acts ch.10 v1-2

But he was not a Jew and so far only the Jews had the good news about Jesus and what he came to do.

On day about three in the afternoon he had a vision. He distinctly saw an angel of God ... "Now send men to Joppa to bring back a man named Simon who is called Peter." Acts ch.10 v3, v5

Simon Peter went there to Cornelius a centurion.

As I (Peter) began to speak, the Holy Spirit come on them as he had come on us at the beginning ... God has granted even the Gentiles repentance unto life. Acts ch.11 v15, v18

King Herod was struck down by God and the word of God continued to grow.

Herod went from Judea to Caesarea and stayed there for while … On the appointed day Herod, wearing his royal robes, sat on his throne and delivered a public address to the people. They shouted, "This is the voice of a god, not of a man." Immediately, because Herod did not give praise to God, an angel of the Lord struck him down, and he was eaten by worms and died. But the word of God continued to increase and spread. Acts ch.12 v19, v21-24

The church continued to strengthen or broaden and extend or grow.

Paul wanted to go to Caesarea on his second missionary journey:

Then he set sail from Ephesus. When he landed at Caesarea, he went up and greeted the church and then went down to Antioch. Acts ch.18 v21-22

On his third missionary journey Paul went to Caesarea.

Leaving the next day, we reached Caesarea and stayed at the house of Philip the evangelist, one of the Seven. He had four unmarried daughters who prophesised. After we had been there a number of days, a prophet named Agabus came down from Judea. Acts ch.21 v8-10

This was a lively church who was well established in the word of God. There were prophets and an evangelist who were well received by the church.

THE ABSENT CHURCH IN CAPERNAUM

A city on the north-west shore on the Sea of Galilee. It was an important city with a tax collector and there was a Roman post nearby. There were two possible sites, Tell Hum and Khan Minya and there is less than three miles between them. This is a site of some significance having a town of size and importance.

Jesus had finished saying all this in the hearing of the people, he entered Capernaum. There was a centurion's servant, whom his master valued highly, was sick and about to die. Luke ch.7 v1-2

Jesus was teaching the Jews, about love for enemies, judging others, a tree and its fruit the wise and foolish builders. It is the Sermon on the Mount with Jesus teaching the crowd (see Matthew ch.5 - ch.7).

He said this while teaching in the synagogue in Capernaum. John ch.6 v59

Jesus was talking about the bread of life but many disciples deserted Jesus because they were finding it difficult to accept it.

Jesus said, "It will be more bearable for Tyre and Sidon at the judgement than for you. And you, Capernaum, will you be lifted up to the skies? No, you will go down to the depths." Luke ch.10 v14-15

Even Jesus had problems because of the word he spoke, most of them rejected his sayings.

He who listens to you listens to me; he who rejects you rejects me; but he who rejects me rejects him who sent me. Luke ch.10 v16

There is not a trace of the church, the whole city was gone. Beware that you don't reject God's message. It is a big town, but the people there were not prepared or willing to listen to what Jesus said. Even the Sermon on the Mount didn't convince the people to have a church there. Jesus preached the gospel and nobody responded.

The Church in Jerusalem

Palestine has been the only link between Europe and Asia on the north and Africa on the south side. She was a poor country, but she was constantly enriched by trade and commerce passing through her territory. There were two main routes bordering Palestine: The King's Highway and the Via Maris alongside the Mediterranean Sea.

In the Old Testament times there were agricultural products (sheep, horses, camels) and metals (iron, copper) and timber, textiles and salt (see Ezekiel ch.27 v12-24).

In the New Testament times, trade and commerce are relatively small because the coast of Palestine has no natural harbour on the Mediterranean Sea. Caravan routes converged on Palestine but this was small trade. Most trade depended upon the Romans. State interference with trade and this was not popular with the Jews. Roman trade extended far beyond the boundaries of the empire (Germany, India and China).

An Alexander ship for the transport of Egyptian grain, probably under charter for the Roman government, give a vivid picture of the hazards of trade and navigation (see Acts ch.27 v13-44).

The church was started in Jerusalem when Jesus was risen and taken up into heaven. Jesus gave this command before he was taken away,

"Do not leave Jerusalem, but wait for the gift my Father promised, which you have heard me speak about. For John baptised with water, but in a few days you will be baptised with the Holy Spirit. Acts ch.1 v4-5

It was made up of Jesus' believers or disciples.

They all joined together constantly in prayer, along with the women and Mary the mother of Jesus, and with his brothers. Acts ch.1 v14

It was the prayer to God, constantly all joined together.

Those who accepted his (Peter's) message were baptised, and about three thousand were added to their number that day. Acts ch.2 v41

The task of the early church.

They devoted themselves to the apostles teaching and to fellowship, to the breaking of bread and to prayer. Everyone was filled with awe, and many wonders and signs were done by the apostles. All the believers were together and had everything in common. Selling their possessions and goods, they gave to anyone as he had need. Every day they continued to meet together in the temple courts. They broke bread in their homes and ate together with glad and sincere hearts, praising God and enjoying the favour of all the people. The Lord added to their number daily those who were being saved. Acts ch.2 v42-47

It was faith and deeds. Faith being instructed by the apostles, deeds selling their possessions and giving to the poor.

What kind of work would they be doing?

They devoted themselves to the apostles' teaching.

The fellowship each day in the temple courts.

The breaking bread in their homes and to prayer.

The had one purpose, selling their possessions and goods.

They gave to anyone who had need.

The favour of all the people was with them.

They baptised every day those who were being saved.

The choosing of the seven because of the widows and they are known to be fully of the Spirit and wisdom. The apostles will turn this responsibility over to them, will give our attention to prayer and the ministry of the word (see Acts ch.6 v2-4).

They presented these men to the apostles, who prayed and laid their hands on them. Acts ch.6 v6

It is well known that the seven men all had Greek sounding names. So those elected had a special care to represent their interests fairly and usefully.

So the word of God spread. The number of disciples in Jerusalem increased rapidly, and a large number of priests became obedient to the faith. Acts ch.6 v7

Every day, God would add to the believers, those who were being saved. This is the beginning of the church that Jesus formed. A large number of priests were in the church there. But they were priests, not apostles and not even elders.

THE CHURCH IN GALILEE

This part of north Palestine, which was the scene of Jesus' boyhood and early ministry. Surrounded on three sides by non-Jewish populations. Bordered by the Jordan valley and cut off from the Mediterranean Sea by the Syro Phoenicia down the coastal path. This was an upland area going up to a thousand feet, bordered on all the sides except the north it was fertile lands and wild plains.

When the Feast of Pentecost came around, some Jews heard them talking not of Greek, but accents where they came from, the parts of the empire.

Utterly amazed, they asked: "Are not all these men who are speaking Galileans? Then how is it that each of us hears them in his own native language?" Acts ch.2 v7-8

After Stephen had been killed most of the church in Jerusalem was scattered and some went to Galilee.

Then the church throughout Judea, Galilee and Samaria enjoyed a time of peace. It was strengthened; and encouraged by the Holy Spirit, it grew in numbers, living in the fear of the Lord. Acts ch.9 v31

Galilee was strengthen by God and it grew in numbers. The church in the districts of Judea, Galilee and Samaria are all one. Focusing on what the Lord Jesus had decided.

Peter said, "I now realise how true it is that God does not show favouritism but accepts men from every nation who fear him and do what is right ... You know that has happened throughout Judea, beginning in Galilee after the baptism that John (the Baptist) preached." Acts ch.10 v34-35, v37

Simon Peter had a vision and the Holy Spirit said to him, "Go with them." He went to Cornelius house for he was a centurion in Caesarea but he was a Gentile and not a Jew.

God does not show favouritism because of his station on life, his nationality or his material possessions. He does however, respect his character and judge his work. Cornelius lacked faith in Jesus Christ so that's why Peter was sent to him.

THE CHURCH IN JOPPA

It was a walled town and it served as an early seaport for Jerusalem. It is the only natural harbour between the bay of Acco and the Egyptian frontier. It became a centre for piracy and during the Jewish War. Emperor Vespasian attacked and captured it. It became known as Jaffa and is a suburb of Tel Aviv.

Peter went to Joppa.

In Joppa there was a disciple named Tabitha (which, when translated, is Dorcas), who was always doing good and helping the poor. About that time, she became sick and died, and her body was washed and placed in an upstairs room. Acts ch.9 v36-37

A good person who cared for the poor. If burial was delayed it was normal to place the body in an upstairs room.

All the widows stood around him (Peter), crying and showing him the robes and other clothing that Dorcas had made while she was still with them. Acts ch.9 v39

Peter sent them out of the room then he got down on his knees and prayed. The prayer was answered and Dorcas opened her eyes. He took her by the hand and helped her to her feet. Peter had seen Jesus raise the dead three times (Matthew ch.9 v25, Luke ch.7 v11-17 and John ch.11 v1-44). Unlike Jesus, Peter got down on his knees and prayed.

Peter stayed in Joppa for some time with a tanner named Simon. Acts ch.9 v43

It is a place near the sea. But Peter had a vision, he went up on the roof to pray and he became hungry and wanted something to eat. While the meal was being prepared he fell into a trance. Peter left Joppa to go to Casearea for a centurion had called him and that is what the vision meant.

There were believers in Joppa and Peter went there to help the church.

The Church in Lydda

Lydda was on the route from Jerusalem to Joppa where the foothills merge into the Plain of Sharon. It is almost certain to be identified with the Old Testament, Lod. It was burnt down in Emperor Nero's reign. After the fall of Jerusalem, it became a rabbinical centre for a period of time.

Peter went to Lydda.

As Peter travelled about the country, he went to visit the saints in Lydda. Acts ch.9 v32

'Saints' is an unusual word, as having lived a life of holiness and exceptional virtue, a person of outstanding kindness. A likely place to have received the early Christian witness.

Peter said to him (a paralytic who had been bedridden for eight years), "Jesus Christ heals you. Get up and tidy up your mat." Immediately Aeneas got up. All those is Lydda and Sharon saw him and turned to the Lord. Acts ch.9 v34-35

All those who saw him believed in the Lord.

The Church in Samaria

The city was colonised by the Greeks after its capture by Alexander the Great. It was left to Herod to embellish the city which he renamed in honour of his Emperor Augustus. There was a fortification wall, three round towers and a palace.

Philip went down to Samaria.

Those who had been scattered (in Jerusalem) preached the word wherever they went. Philip went down to a city in Samaria and proclaimed the Christ there. When the crowds heard Philip and saw the miraculous signs he did, they all paid close attention to what he said. Acts ch.8 v4-6

He preached the good news of the kingdom of God, and they were baptised, both men and women. Simon himself believed and was baptised, but he was a sorcerer and had practised in the town of Samaria.

When the apostles in Jerusalem heard that Samaria had accepted the word of God, they sent Peter and John to them. Acts ch.8 v14

They prayed for them, that they might receive the Holy Spirit. But Simon the sorcerer offered them money so he could practice this. Peter said, "Repent of this wickedness and pray to God for I see that you are not right before God." They didn't cast him out of the church, even though he was a sorcerer. Simon answered, "Pray to the Lord for me."

When they had testified and proclaimed the word of the Lord, Peter and John returned to Jerusalem, preaching the gospel in many Samaritan villages. Acts ch.8 v25

Then the church throughout Judea, Galilee and Samaria enjoyed a time of peace. Acts ch.9 v31

The church (in Antioch) sent them on their way, and as they travelled through Phoenicia and Samaria, they told how the Gentiles had been converted. The news made all the brothers very glad. Acts ch.15 v3

The town in Samaria was not Jews but Gentiles. The Jews weren't there, because there was a lot of religious envy (see 2 Kings ch.17 v24-41).

"You are a Jew and I am a Samaritan woman. How can you ask me for a drink?" (For Jews do not associate with Samaritans.) John ch.4 v9

Paul and Barnabas on their first missionary journey were asked to go up to Jerusalem to see the apostles and elders and to determine the whole question about what to do with the Gentile Christians. It formed a Council at Jerusalem (see Acts ch.15 v1-35).

The Church in Sharon

It comprises the largest of the coastal plains in northern Palestine. From Joppa to Casearea and is only ten miles wide for the strip of land. Formerly this area was thickly forested with oak trees and is one of the richest agricultural districts of Israel, planted with citrus groves. Only the southern border of Sharon was suitable for inhabitants.

Peter was in the plains of Sharon.

It was most likely Aeneas who was one of the believers (see Acts ch.9 v32-34).

All those who lived in ... Sharon saw him and turned to the Lord. Acts ch.9 v35

Syria

The Church in Antioch

Built at the foot of Mount Sylphus, it overlooked the navigable river Orontes and boasted a fine seaport. Antioch fell to Emperor Pompey and he made it a 'free city'. Subsequently, it became the capital of the Roman province of Syria and was the largest city of the Empire. Apart from Jerusalem itself, no other city could match itself with the connections of the beginning of Christianity.

The believers had already been to Antioch and preached the word. Other Jews probably fled to Antioch during the Macceabean wars. The revolt against Rome fearing that an attempt to desecrate the Temple.

After Stephen had been killed the believers in Jerusalem scattered.

Now those who had been scattered by the persecution in connection with Stephen travelled as far as Phoenicia, Cyprus and Antioch, telling the message only to Jews. Acts ch.11 v19

Only for the Jews and definitely not the Greeks and Barbarians.

The Lord's hand was with them, and a great number of people believed and turned to the Lord. News of this reached the ears of the church at Jerusalem, and they sent Barnabas to Antioch. Acts ch.11 v21-22

Barnabas went to Tarsus to look for Paul, he brought him to Antioch and for a whole year they met with the church and taught great numbers of people (see Acts ch.11 v25-26).

The disciples were called Christians first at Antioch. Acts ch.11 v26

During this time some prophets came down from Jerusalem to Antioch. One of them named Agabus stood up and predicted that a severe famine would spread over the Roman world. The disciples decided to provide help for the brothers living in Judea and they sent their gift to the elders there (see Acts ch.11 v27-30).

In Pisidian Antioch, named after the death of Antiochus, King of Syria. It was one hundred miles away and was situated on an important trading route between Ephesus and Cilicia. It was a different place from Syrian Antioch.

In the church at Antioch there were prophets and teachers ... While they were worshipping the Lord and fasting, the Holy Spirit said, "Set apart for my Barnabas and Paul for the work to which I have called them." Acts ch.13 v1-2

The start of Paul and Barnabas first missionary journey.

From Attalia they sailed back to Antioch, where they had been committed to the grace of God for the word they had now completed. On arriving there, they gathered the church together and reported all that God had done through them and how he had opened the door of faith to the Gentiles. Acts ch.14 26-27

They were there for some long time.

Some men came down from Judea to Antioch and were teaching the brothers. Acts ch.15 v1

Paul and Barnabas had a sharp dispute among them, believing that the Gentiles were free from Jewish laws and didn't have to go through circumcision. So, Paul and Barnabas and others were sent to the Council of Jerusalem.

When Peter came to Antioch he used to eat with the Gentiles. But when certain men came from James, he drew back and separated himself from the Gentiles because he was afraid of those who belonged to the circumcision group. The other Jews joined him in this hypocrisy, even Barnabas was led astray (see Galatians ch.2 v11-13).

The whole assembly (in Jerusalem) became silent as they listened to Barnabas and Paul telling about the miraculous signs and wonders God had done among the Gentiles through them. Acts ch.15 v12

James who was leader of the church in Jerusalem was going to write a letter to Antioch: It is not reasonable for the Gentiles who are turning to God, telling them to abstain from food sacrificed to idols, from sexual immorality and from the meat of strangled animals and blood.

Then the apostles and elders, with the whole church, decided to choose some of their own men and send them to Antioch with Paul and Barnabas. Acts ch.15 v22

The people read it and were glad for its encouraging message. Judas and Silas, who themselves were prophets, said much to encourage and strengthen the brothers ... but Paul and Barnabas remained in Antioch, where they and many others taught and preached the word of the Lord. Acts ch.15 v31-32, v35

The whole issue whether the Gentiles and Jews were still present after James sent his letter, because the Jews maintained that the Gentiles conformed to the practice of the Jews, likely the circumcision group. Paul maintained his position and said,

For sin shall not be your master, because you are not under law, but under grace. Romans ch.6 v14

On Paul and Silas second missionary journey around Asia.

While Paul and Silas completed their second missionary in Asia he returned to Antioch (see Acts ch.18 v22-23)

Paul said to Timothy,

You, however, know all about my teaching, my way of life, my purpose, faith, patience, love, endurance, persecutions, sufferings - what kinds of things happened to me to Antioch, Iconium and Lystra, the persecutions I endured. Yet the Lord rescued me from all of them. 2 Timothy ch.3 v10-11

Paul had problems in Antioch where he spent considerable time and effort trying to persuade both the Jews and Gentiles to get along together.

The Church in Damascus

Saul was there giving approval for the death of Stephen in Jerusalem (see Acts ch.8 v1).

Saul was still breathing out murderous threats against the Lord's disciples. He went to the high priest and asked for letters to the synagogues in Damascus, so that if he found any there who belonged to the Way, whether men or women, he might take them as prisoners to Jerusalem. Acts ch.9 v1-2

Saul met Jesus before he arrived in Damascus but he was a broken man. Jesus called him from heaven, saying, "Why do you persecute me?" It was Jesus, not the disciples of the Lord he treated abominably hounding them up to take them to Jerusalem as prisoners.

In Damascus there was a disciple named Ananias ... Saul spent several days with the disciples in Damascus. At once he began to preach in the synagogues that Jesus is the Son of God. Acts ch.9 v10, v19-20

It was a marked change for Saul. He didn't try to hide himself away from the Jews, he went and preached in the synagogues that Jesus was king of all.

Saul was an educated man, more powerful and baffled the Jews living in Damascus by proving that Jesus is the Christ (see Acts ch.9 v22). So the Jews thought they stop him, by going to the king in Damascus they guarded the gate to the city. Saul was also called Paul (see Acts ch.13 v9).

In Damascus the governor under King Aretas had the city of the Damascenes guarded in order to arrest me. But I was lowered in a basket from a window is the wall and slipped though his hands. 2 Corinthians ch.11 v32-33

When he came to Jerusalem, he tried to join the disciples. But they were afraid of him, so Barnabas took him and brought him to the apostles.

Paul went immediately into Arabia and later returned to Damascus. Galatians ch.1 v17

Paul went into Damascus to help and support the believers. Particularly Ananias who helped him to see, after Paul met Jesus on the road to Damascus.

On Paul's fourth missionary journey to Rome.

I was not disobedient to the vision from heaven. First to those in Damascus, then to those in Jerusalem and in all Judea and to the Gentiles also, I preached that they should repent and turn to God and prove their repentance by their deeds. Acts ch.26 v19-20

THE ABSENT CHURCH IN MESOPOTAMIA

This was the fertile land east of the Orontes and the Euphrates Rivers, the lands watered by the Habur and Tigris Rivers. The Greek and Roman writers extended the use of Mesopotamia to cover the modern state of Iraq. This may explain that the Jews in Babylon were present at the Feast of Pentecost.

Parthians, Medes and Elamites: residents of Mesopotamia. Acts ch.2 v9

Stephen one of the seven, argued to the Sanhedrin:

The God of glory appeared to our father Abraham while he was still living in Mesopotamia, before he lived Haran. "Leave your country and your people," God said, "and go to the land I will show you." Acts ch.7 v2-3

While Abraham was still living in Mesopotamia he was told to go to the land of Canaan, further west and down south by the Mediterranean Sea.

It was still far beyond Antioch, much further than Babylon and I am not sure that Paul on his missionary journeys reached there. Still the Jews will come back to the Feast of Pentecost in Jerusalem.

Peter preached Jesus at the Feast of Pentecost.

Those who accepted Peter's message were baptised, and about three thousand were added to their number that day. Acts ch.2 v41

There was a mix of people in Jerusalem and some were in Mesopotamia far away. There is no evidence that Mesopotamia had a church there.

The Church in Phoenicia

The territory on the Mediterranean Sea between the Litani and Arvad Rivers. The place is located on the principle cites, like Sidon and Tyre. There was extensive trade in timber between Phoenicia and Egypt and supplying fish to Jerusalem.

Be silent, you people of the island and you merchants of Sidon, whom the seafarers have enriched. On the great waters came the grain of the Shihor; the harvest of the Nile was the revenue of Tyre, and she became the market-place of the nations. Isaiah ch.23 v2-3

When Stephen is killed by stoning of the Jews there was a great persecution in Jerusalem.

Now those who had been scattered by the persecution in connection with Stephen, travelled as far as Phoenicia ... telling the message only to Jews. Acts ch.11 v19

The believers are scattered by the suffering and persecution that followed. Even going to Cyprus, away from their families. In the early days of the church, only the Jews had the message of the kingdom of God. Later the Gentiles had been converted.

Paul and Barnabas on there first missionary journey.

The church sent them on their way, and as they travelled through Phoenicia and Samaria, they told how the Gentiles had been converted. This news made all the brothers very glad. Acts ch.15 v3

They came to Phoenicia and the news was well received in Jerusalem.

Paul on his third missionary journey.

We (Paul and others) landed at Tyre, where our ship was to unload its cargo. Finding the disciples there, we stayed with them several days. Through the Spirit they urged Paul not to go on to Jerusalem. Acts ch.21 v3-4

At Tyre knowing that Paul was going up to the Feast of Pentecost. The Spirit warned of the coming trials in store for Paul at Jerusalem; the disciples had a prophet with them and alerted him not to go. But Paul was certain to go, even if he might be captured.

THE CHURCH IN PTOLEMAIS

The seaport of Accho, on the north point of the Bay of Acre. During the Old Testament the name was changed to Ptolemais, presumably in honour of Ptolemy Philadelphus. The Emperor Claudius having settled a group of veterans there. It was the only natural harbour on the coast south of Phoenicia and various routes connected with Galilee Sea and the Jordan valley.

Paul on his third missionary journey.

We (Paul and others) continued our voyage from Tyre and landed at Ptolemais, where we greeted the brothers and stayed with them for a day. Acts ch.21 v7

Paul was heading to Jerusalem to the Feast of Pentecost. They were only there for a day and they met with the believers at Ptolemais. There was a church there.

THE CHURCH IN TYRE

The principle seaport on the Phoenician coast, it comprised two harbours. The city was fed by water by the River Litani and dominated the surrounding plain. Alexander the Great laid siege to the city for seven months and captured it despite heavy losses, because the city was surrounded by many walls. The magnificent places had been a source of cultural seductiveness and religious idolatry since the time of Jezebel (see 1 Kings ch.18 v19).

Before Paul's missionary journeys.

They (the people of Tyre) … asked for peace, because they depended on the king's country for their food supply. Acts ch.12 v20

They were dependent on their fields of Galilee for their food. They didn't want to upset Herod who managed the fields and they asked Blastus a trusted personal servant of the king.

Paul third missionary journey.

We landed at Tyre, where our ship was to unload its cargo. Finding the disciples there, we stayed with them for seven days. Through the Spirit they urged Paul not to go on to Jerusalem. But when our time was up, we left and continued on our way. All the disciples and their wives and children accompanied us out of the city, and there on the beach we knelt to pray. Acts ch.21 v3-5

Paul was heading up to Jerusalem. There was a church there in the city of Tyre with many wives and their children. Paul knew his time had come and was going up to the Jerusalem for the last time. He knew he was going to be imprisoned.

ARABIA

THE ABSENT CHURCH IN ARABIA

The structure of Arabian consists of a mass of rocks form a range of mountain on the west, rising about 10,000 feet in places. Where the annual rainfall exceeds twenty inches, people were settled there where irrigation is practicable. In the whole of the rest of the area the annual rainfall is negligible and life depends of oases and wells. Its a hard place to visit.

Paul had a lot of thinking to do. Finding out he was a Jew trained, educated man and then he was called by Jesus to help with the Gentiles. Who were hated by the Jews (see John ch.4 v9), because they didn't follow the ways of the Lord (see 2 Kings ch.17 v24-41).

When God, who set me apart from birth and called me by his grace, was pleased to reveal his Son in me that I might preach him among the Gentiles, I did not consult any man, nor did I go up to Jerusalem to see those who were apostles before I was, but I went immediately into Arabia and later returned to Damascus. Galatians ch.1 v15-17

God chose Paul before he was born, but he did not go up to Jerusalem. Why? Because it relies on God's help for rainfall, there is a lot of desert there without any shrubs or trees.

The gospel I preached is not something that man made up. I did not receive it from any man, nor was I taught it; rather, I received it by revelation from Jesus Christ. Galatians ch.1 v11-12

There are only two options for mankind: one of which is slavery to sin, the other is called by God to be free from sin. This is why Paul made sure that the word he received from God is not made by human intellect (see Romans ch.5 v12-21).

There is no mention of a church in Arabia; but the Israelites went to Mount Sinai and Paul went there to reflect. It is basically out of the way. You will have to think about what faith means; he was there for some while.

Egypt

The Church in Alexandria

A seaport on the coast of the Egyptian Delta whose entrance was dominated by the Tower of Pharos. It was founded in 332 BC by Alexandria the Great and named after himself. The city was apparently laid out with a grid pattern of streets. Alexandria was a cosmopolitan city, with a library and museum and a stadium. Besides the Greek citizens there was a very large Jewish community.

Opposition arose, however, from members of the Synagogue of the Freedman (as it was called) - Jews of Cyrene and Alexandria as well as the provinces of Cilicia and Asia. These men began to argue with Stephen. Acts ch.6 v9

When Stephen among the Seven was chosen to overlook or oversee the Hebraic Jewish widows in the daily distribution of food in the early church. We don't know what they were arguing about, it probably had to do with the Grecian Jews.

Paul was on his third missionary journey.

Meanwhile a Jew named Apollos, a native of Alexandria ... He was a learned man, with a thorough knowledge of the Scriptures. He had been instructed in the way of the Lord, and he spoke with great fervour and taught about Jesus accurately, though he knew only the baptism of John (the Baptist). Acts ch.18 v24-25

Apollos did not really understand about Jesus, what he taught and his miracles in Judah. But he knew that Jesus had been killed by crucifixion in Jerusalem. When Priscilla and Aquila heard him, they invited him into their home and explained to him the way of God more adequately, more suitable and acceptable (see Acts ch.18 v26).

Paul was on his forth missionary journey to Rome.

There the centurion found an Alexandrian ship sailing for Italy and put us on board. Acts ch.27 v6

Paul was as a captive going to meet Caesar, the centurion Julius found an Alexandrian ship. But it was later in the year and unfortunately, the ship was destroyed by the hurricane called the 'north-easter'. The owner and the pilot of the ship didn't understand the weather (see Acts ch.27 v11). The ship was caught by the storm and could not head into it. However, all the sailors, soldiers and captives survived and they arrived on the island of Malta (see Acts ch.27 v13-44).

The Church in Cyrene

A port in North Africa rich in corn, wool and dates. It was bequeathed to Rome for it was a Ptolemaic Empire and became a Roman province. There was a Jewish settlement.

Egypt and the parts of Libya near Cyrene. Acts ch.2 v10

When the Feast of Pentecost came round in Jerusalem the disciples were filled with the Holy Spirit. There was a lot of Jews visiting at the Feast, each of them hearing the words in his own native language.

Stephen was later hauled into the Sanhedrin to speak about what he did. In the verses, the first place was the Jews in Cyrene.

Opposition arose, however, from members of the Synagogue of the Freedman (as it was called) - Jews of Cyrene and Alexandria. Acts ch.6 v9

It was a turning point for the church in Jerusalem. There were many people in the city apart form the disciples, and it was needed for them to go out witnessing to the people from the nations around them.

Those who had been scattered by the persecution in connection with Stephen .... some of them, however, men from Cyprus and Cyrene, went to Antioch and began to speak to the Greeks also, telling them the good news about the Lord Jesus. The Lord's hand was with them, and a great number of people believed and turned to the Lord. Acts ch.11 v19-21

They went out proclaiming the word of the Lord and a great number of people believed and turned to the Lord. This was the start of what the Lord had instructed the people to do (see Matthew ch.28 v18-20).

It wasn't Paul, but it was the believers going to Antioch before Paul and Barnabas had been called by the Holy Spirit. They followed Jesus precisely. This is the reason that the Jews and the Gentiles were indeed happy in the church.

The Holy Spirit called Paul and Barnabas to go out on their first missionary journey.

In the church of Antioch there were prophets and teachers ... Lucius of Cyrene. Acts ch.13 v1

He was a prophet and a teacher in Antioch but he came from Cyrene.

THE CHURCH IN EGYPT

The area of Egypt goes from the Mediterranean Sea with a total surface area of over 350,000 miles. However, of this whole area only 96% is desert and only 4% usable for land, where the River Nile feeds its way to the Mediterranean Sea.

Alexandria has barely seven and-a-half inches of rain each year, and Cairo just over one inch. For life-giving water Egypt depends wholly on the River Nile.

At the Feast of Pentecost.

Egypt and parts of Lybia near Cyrene; visitors from Rome (both Jews and converts to Judaism). Acts ch.2 v10

But there were still Jews and converts to Judaism in Egypt. It is a long way to go to Jerusalem, over the Wilderness of Paran, but there were two roads between Egypt and Palestine.

Peter said, "Save yourself from this corrupt generation." Those who accepted his message were baptised, and about three thousand were added to their number that day. Acts ch.2 v40-41

When he spoke to the crowds there and about some people responded to his message.

When Jesus was born, his father Joseph received a dream telling him the boy was in danger and to go down to Egypt where he would be safe (see Matthew ch.2 v13-15). There was likely to be believers there because he stayed for some while until Herod was dead.

The Church in Ethiopia

Ethiopia refers to the kingdom of Candace, who ruled at Meroe where the capital had been moved during the Persian period. This was not unusual for a high-official, a royal treasurer in the court of Queen Candace to rise above the harem attendants.

Philip was called to go out to a desert road by an angel of the Lord.

This man had gone to Jerusalem to worship, and on his way home was sitting in his chariot reading the book of Isaiah the prophet. Acts ch.8 v27-28

The eunuch had gone to Jerusalem to worship the Lord and he had a chariot which marked him out as important.

The eunuch asked Philip, "Tell me, please, who is the prophet talking about, himself or someone else?" Then Philip began with that very same passage of Scripture and told him the good news about Jesus. Acts ch.8 v34-35

The desert road that goes down from Jerusalem to Gaza (see Acts ch.8 v26). God knew he was going back to his home and he sent Philip to meet him.

Look, here is water, Why shouldn't I be baptised? Acts ch.8 v37

He was an important and significant man, he asked Philip to baptise him.

When they came up out of the water, the Spirit of the Lord suddenly took Philip away, and the eunuch did not see him again, but went on his way rejoicing. Acts ch.8 v39

There was a lot of people all around the eunuch and the two of them went down in the water to baptise him. People helping him up out of the water giving him clothing, helping him to go on to the chariot. This is why Philip quietly was taken away.

We know that the eunuch went back to Ethiopia and told many people about the word of the Lord. But we don't read anything more about Ethiopia in the verses of Scripture. He met with God and believed.

The eunuch didn't realise how much value he was worth, that even Philip was directed by an angel of the Lord and sent for him to be saved.

CYPRUS

THE CHURCH IN PAPHOS

It was a Phoenician town lying slightly inland from the coast. After the Romans took over the island as the centre of Roman rule. Paphos was the site of a famous shrine but later devoted to the worship of Aphrodite.

Paul's and Barnabas first missionary journey.

They travelled through the whole island until they came to Paphos. There they met a Jewish sorcerer and false prophet named Bar-Jesus, who was an attendant of the proconsul, Sergius Paulus. Acts ch.13 v6-7

They went on their way by the Holy Spirit and visited Cyprus. A proconsul was the title of a governor because they did not need a standing army or soldiers.

Immediately mist and darkness came over him (Bar-Jesus), and he groped about, seeking someone to lead him by the hand. When the proconsul saw what had happened, he believed, for he was amazed at the teaching about the Lord. Acts ch.13 v11-12

This was one of the believers, but he didn't follow what Jesus had done for him - Jesus was blinded and sought someone to take him by the hand. The proconsul believed because he saw what the power of God could do. Paul and Silas would explain to him the teaching of the Lord Jesus.

The Absent Church in Salamis

A town on the east coast of the central plain of Cyrus. It rivalled in importance to Paphos, the Roman capital of the whole island. Eventually superseded it. The harbour which made Salamis a great commercial centre is now completely silted up. Destroyed by earthquakes as the town was rebuilt as Constantia.

Paul and Barnabas on their first missionary journey.

When they arrived at Salamis, they proclaimed the word of God in the Jewish synagogues. John was with them as their helper. Acts ch.13 v5

They went to Cyprus, because Barnabas had a home there.

For instance, there was Joseph, the one the apostles nicknamed Barnabas (which means "Son of Encouragement"). He was from the tribe of Levi and came from the island of Cyprus. Acts ch.4 v36 (NLT)

There is no evidence that there were believers there. The proconsul in Paphos and he was an intelligent man because he wanted to here about the word of God. In his responsibility he would do something about it. But we don't know what he did. There could have been a church there.

Barnabas and Mark went to Cyprus.

Barnabas took (John who is also called) Mark and sailed for Cyprus. Acts ch.15 v39

Barnabas was committed to Cyprus because he wanted the churches to grow. When he argued with Paul, they had such a 'sharp disagreement' about the work still to be done. Barnabas took Mark and went back to Cyprus.

There is no evidence about what he did for Cyprus. Most of the apostles what they did for the Lord is not recorded in any of the Bible. The book of the Acts focuses on Paul.

But he doesn't seem to have been effective. For there is no other churches around. Only the church in Paphos. He might have gone back to where his home was.

Asia Minor

The Church in Bithynia

A territory on the Asiatic side of the Bosporus and subsequently administered with Pontus as a single Roman province. It is located by the Euxine Sea and is close to Heroclea that is a town.

On the second journey of Paul and Silas going through Asia Minor.

When they (Paul and Silas) came to the border of Mysia, they tried to enter Bithynia, but the Spirit of Jesus would not allow them to (enter). Acts ch.16 v7

The Holy Spirit may have led them in many different ways: vision, circumstances, good sense or use of prophetic gift. Certainly they didn't enter there, going near the Black Sea or visiting Macedonia (Greece).

In Peter's letters.

Peter, an apostle of Jesus Christ, to God's elect, strangers in the world, scattered through Pontus, Galatia, Cappadocia, Asia and Bithynia, who have been chosen according to the foreknowledge of God the Father, and through the sanctifying work of the Spirit. 1 Peter ch.1 v1-2

He reminded the church to encourage the people there, testifying that this is the true grace of God. 'Stand fast in it' (see 1 Peter ch.5 v12).

In this you greatly rejoice, though now for a little while you may have to suffer grief in all kinds of trials. 1 Peter ch.1 v6.

The church must have had those who suffered for belonging to Jesus.

THE CHURCH IN CAPPADOCIA

A highland province in the east of Asia Minor. On the south by the mountains of Mount Taurus, on the east by the Euphrates River and north by the area of Pontus. Under the Emperor Trajon the size and importance of the province greatly increased as it produced large numbers of sheep and horses.

When the Feast of Pentecost arrived, people were in Jerusalem a journey through the land of some six hundred miles. It would take some expedition with bandits and robbers hiding in the hills.

At the Feast of Pentecost.

Now there were staying in Jerusalem God-fearing Jews from every nation under heaven ... Cappadocia (was mentioned). Acts ch.2 v5, v9

There were God-fearing Jews including Cappadocia and they travelled as far as Jerusalem at the Feast of Pentecost and there's no mention of them taking horses with them.

In Peters letters.

To God's elect, strangers in the world ... Cappadocia ... who have been chosen according to the foreknowledge of God the Father, through the sanctifying work of the Spirit. 1 Peter ch.1 v1-2

There were believers there as in Bithynia but in Scripture we don't hear much about it.

THE CHURCH IN COLOSSE

A city in the Roman province of Asia Minor. It was situated on the main road from Ephesus to the east. But under the Romans its importance waned, partly because the road to Pergamum was resited further west and Laodicea became the larger and more prosperous city. The site in now uninhabited.

Paul third missionary journey.

Paul, and apostle of Christ Jesus by the will of God, and Timothy our brother, to the holy and faithful brothers in Christ at Colosse. Colossians ch.1 v1-2

There were believers the holy and faithful brothers there.

Epaphras: What gave Colosse importance however, during Paul's ministry in Ephesus. Epaphras had been converted and had carried the gospel to Colosse. The young church had become the target of sustained attack.

This went on for two years, so that all the Jews and Greeks who lived in the province of Asia heard the word of the Lord. Acts ch.19 v10

It will be a long time for two whole years all the Jews and Greeks in Asia heard the gospel. It was amazing that Paul worked diligently, hard for them to convince the people that they should look to Jesus as their Saviour and Lord.

You learned it from Epaphras, our dear fellow-servant, who is a faithful minister of Christ on our behalf, and has told us of your love in the Spirit. Colossians ch.1 v7-8

Even Epaphras has convinced the Colosse church of their love for the Lord. By carrying it around with him and speaking to the people there for his faith.

See to it that no-one takes you captive through hollow and deceptive philosophy, which depends on human tradition and the basic principles of this world rather than on Christ. Colossians ch.2 v8

They were arguing about human traditions which depend on the basic principles of this world. We should be focusing on Jesus and what he has done though his miracles, teaching and death on the cross. To be raised again and went up to heaven.

Human traditions leads to 'do not handle, do not taste, do not touch' (see Colossians ch.2 v21). This is not what we should be doing. Going out talking to people about the Lord Jesus Christ (see Matthew ch.28 v19-20).

The Church in Derbe

A city of the Lycaonian region of Roman Galatia, the most easterly place visited by Paul and Barnabas while they preached the message on their first missionary journey. Further east would have taken them beyond the Roman province into the kingdom of Antiochus.

At Iconium, there was a riot by the Jews and Gentiles. The people of the city were divided, some settled for what Paul had been saying, others were only for the Jews and what things they wanted.

On Paul and Barnabas first missionary journey to Lystra.

But they found out about it and fled to the Lycaonian cities of Lystra and Derbe and to the surrounding country, where they continued to preach the good news. Acts ch.14 v6-7

Paul in Lystra did a miraculous sign and they all thought that the gods had come to them. Then some Jews won the crowd over. They came from Antioch and Iconium and they stoned Paul, dragged him outside the city walls, thinking that he was dead. But he got up after they finished with him and went back into the city.

Stoning: Was the usual Hebrew form of execution. The prosecution witnesses had to cast the first stone, afterward if the victim lived the other people carried out the sentence and the body was suspended until sunset (see Deuteronomy ch.21 v23). Stones of course were the primary building material. God must have protected Paul; but he was weakened and fell down on the floor.

The next day Paul and Barnabas left for Derbe. They preached the good news in that city and won a large number of disciples. Acts ch.14 v20-21

Later he went back to Lystra and strengthened and encouraged the disciples and Paul said, 'We must go through many hardships to be saved'.

Paul and Barnabas appointed elders for them in each church and, with prayer and fasting, committing them to the Lord, in whom they had put their trust. Acts ch.14 v23

His thought was to appoint elders for them in each church, because the apostles had work to do. With prayer and fasting, committing them to the Lord. The elders had to carry on after the apostles, who were limited to twelve.

Paul and Silas second missionary journey to Lystra.

He came to Derbe and then to Lystra, where a disciple named Timothy lived, whose mother was a Jewess and a believer, but whose father was a Greek. Acts ch.16 v1

Paul and Silas came to Derbe. He was pleased that his church had many disciples, both Jews and Greek. He didn't comment that he was stoned and presumed dead, it was in the past. He selected Timothy to be with him.

On his third missionary journey Paul was on his own.

He was accompanied by ... Gaius from Derbe, Timothy also ... these men went on ahead of us and waited for us at Troas. Acts ch.20 v4-5

Timothy also was a boy and had become a man. We know that Timothy was a true son 'in the faith' (see 1 Timothy ch.1 v2) and he with Paul up until he was in Rome (see 2 Timothy ch.4 v21).

He wrote to Timothy thinking that he was best to serve in the faith after Paul was in prison (see 1 and 2 Timothy).

THE CHURCH IN EPHESUS

The most important city in the Roman province of Asia Minor. Situated on an island harbour, the city was connected by a narrow channel between the mountain ranges of Koressos and the Mediterranean Sea. A magnificent road lined with columns ran down from the city to the fine harbour.

The main part of the city with its theatre, baths, libraries and marble-paved streets, but the temple lay to the north-east. This site for which is sacred to the fertility goddess of Artemis. There was a large colony of Jews at Ephesus and they enjoyed a privileged position under the early empire. However, it is now uninhabited.

Paul made a short visit there on his second missionary journey.

Meanwhile a Jew named Apollos, a native of Alexandria, came to Ephesus. he was a leaned man. Acts ch.18 v24

Christianity came to Ephesus with Aquila and Priscilla, Paul left them there to help the church. They invited Apollos into their home and explained to him the way of God more adequately, they pointed out from the baptism of John the work of Jesus what he taught, his miracles that he performed.

When Apollos wanted to go to Achaia, the brothers encouraged him and wrote to the disciples there to welcome him. On arriving, he was a great help to those who by grace had believed. Acts ch.18 v27

Apollos he was a learned man with a thorough knowledge of the Scriptures and would be a help to the church in Achaia.

On Paul's third missionary journey.

So Paul left them. He took the disciples with him and had discussion daily in the lecture hall of Tyrannus. This went on for two years, so that all the Jews and Greeks who lived in the province of Asia heard about the word of the Lord. Acts ch.19 v9-10

Paul took the road from Corinth and arrived at Ephesus. There he found some disciples. He entered the synagogue and spoke boldly about the kingdom of God, but the Jews refused to believe. Paul left them and took the believers, this went on for about two years and many people heard about Jesus.

When this became known to the Jews and Greeks living in Ephesus, they were all seized with fear, and the name of the Lord Jesus was held in high honour ... In this way the word of the Lord spread widely and grew in power. Acts ch.19 v17, v20

This time a great disturbance in Ephesus. Demetrius who made shrines of Artemis called together the craftsmen and said, The goddess of Artemis will be discredited. All of them were furious and began shouting. The city clerk quietened the crowd and said, 'These men have not robbed temples, nor blasphemed our goddess.'

When the uproar had ended, Paul sent for the disciples and, after encouraging them, said good-bye and set out for Macedonia. Acts ch.20 v1

After this the city clerk dismissed the assembly and Paul left.

From Miletus, Paul sent to Ephesus for the elders of the church. When they arrived, he said to them: "You know how I lived the whole time I was with you, from the first day I came into the province of Asia. I served the Lord with great humility and with tears ... Keep watch over ourselves and al the flock of which the Holy Spirit has made you overseers. Be shepherds of the church of God ... I know that after I leave, savage wolves will come in among you and will not spare the flock. Even from your own number men will arise and distort the truth in order to draw away disciples after them. So be on your guard!" Acts ch.20 v17-19, v28-31

Paul warns the elders to be on the look out for false doctrines to lead men away from the truth. It is in the church there.

It I fought wild beasts in Ephesus for merely human reasons, what have I gained? if the dead are not raised ... Do not be misled, "Bad company corrupts good character." 1 Corinthians ch.15 v32-33

Even for the church in Ephesus which is now in ruins today. Bad company with no effective elders closes the door of the church. They are responsible for guiding the church to hold fast to what Jesus taught.

I will stay on at Ephesus until Pentecost, because a great door for effective word has opened to me, and there are many who oppose me.   1 Corinthians ch.16 v8-9

However, Ephesians does not address any particular error or heresy.   So Paul wrote that the Ephesians might better understand the high goals that God has made for the church.   The church at Ephesus was very good and Paul stayed there for two years.   The church at Ephesus was all happy, glad and things were going smoothly, but there were evil men planted in the church.

Paul, an apostle of Christ Jesus by the will of God.   To the saints in Ephesus, the faithful in Christ Jesus: Grace and mercy to you from God our Father and the Lord Jesus Christ.   Ephesians ch.1 v1-2

Paul remarks that Ephesus was 'faithful in Christ Jesus'.

Paul was in prison in Rome.   He was writing at the end of his life:

He says to Timothy, "Stay in Ephesus so that you may command certain men not to teach false doctrines any longer not to devote themselves to myths and endless genealogies.   These promote controversies rather than God's work - which is by faith."   1 Timothy ch.1 v3-4

There in no mention of the elders. They are not willing to stamp out the false doctrines any longer, they have been sidelined and ineffective.

You know very well in how many ways he helped me in Ephesus. 2 Timothy ch.1 v18

The elders should have been guiding Jesus teachings and the word of the Lord. To let the believers under them to work for the kingdom of heaven. Paul was correct to the elders: 'Be shepherds of the flock that is under you.'

John's letter on the Isle of Patmos.

Jesus said, "I know your deeds, your hard work and your perseverance. I know that you cannot tolerate wicked men, that you have tested those who claim to be apostles but are not, and have found them false ... Yet I hold this against you: You have forsaken your first love. Remember the height from which you have fallen! Repent and do the things you did at first." Revelation ch.2 v2, v4-5

He was the last surviving apostle of the Lord Jesus; he was there because he was holding to the testimony of Jesus (see Revelation ch.1 v9). When John wrote the book of Revelation in about 96 AD, sixty years after Paul went to Ephesus. God remarked about losing their first love and he stated that he would remove their 'lampstand' if the church didn't repent.

They should have been doing, to turn round and do the things they were doing at the start of their faith. Sadly, they are no longer with us; standing proud and firm giving help to the other believers that might come to them.

The Church in Galatia

The kingdom of Galatia of the great inner plateau of Asia Minor, including a large portion of the valley of the Halys River. Galatia became a province of the Romans. Large numbers of Romans, Greeks and Jews were attracted to these location because of their strategic places to live.

Paul and Silas visited on their second missionary journey.

Paul and his companions travelled throughout the region of Phrygia and Galatia, having been kept by the Holy Spirit from preaching the word in the province of Asia. When they came to the border of Mysia, they tried to enter Bithynia, but the Spirit of Jesus would not allow them to. Acts ch.16 v6-7

During the night Paul had a vision of a man in Macedonia or Greece standing and begging him. We therefore got ready to go into Greece to preach the gospel there.

Paul's third missionary journey.

Paul set out from there and travelled from place to place throughout the region of Galatia and Phrygia, strengthening all of the disciples. Acts ch.18 v23

He was able to go up north in the region of Galatia and there he was able to help the disciples. By consolidating and encouraging them.

There were several churches in Galatia and Paul told them how to bring money to help God's people.

Now about the collection for God's people: Do what I told the Galatian churches to do. On the first day of every week, each of you should set aside a sum of money in keeping with his income, saving it up, so that when I come no collections will have to be made. 1 Corinthians ch.16 v1-2

There was a large Jewish presence in Galatia and a number of ceremonial practices were still had a rigorous effect on the church.

To the churches in Galatia: Grace and peace from God and Father and the Lord Jesus Christ, who gave himself for our sins to rescue us from this present evil age, according to the will of our God and Father. Galatians ch.1 v2-4

The Jews insisted that the church should follow their rules, especially circumcision which was a practice only for the Jews and not the Gentiles.

Clearly no-one is justified before God by the law, because, "the righteous will live by faith." Galatians ch.3 v11

We live by faith, so indeed the believers are not subject to the rules of the Jews. We are chosen by God who justifies us, forgives us our weaknesses and makes us right with him.

In Peter's letters.

Peter, an apostle of Jesus Christ, to God's elect, strangers in the world, scattered throughout ... Galatia ... who have been chosen according to the foreknowledge of God the Father. 1 Peter ch.1 v1-2

Even Peter was conscious of this. They had been chosen by God because he had foreknowledge of this and not through works. The believer is totally different from the Jew. The Jew is only interested in the Old Testament but the believer holds to the Old and New Testaments.

The Church in Hierapolis

A city in the Roman province of Asia Minor. It was situated north of Laodicea on the opposite side of the broad valley that was there. The city was constructed around hot springs which were then famed for their medicinal powers. These natural features made Hierapolis a sacred city. There is now only a small village near by; it lies at the foot of spectacular cliffs of lime which have been deposited over the centuries from the hot springs.

The church in Hierapolis was probably founded while Paul was living at Ephesus.

Paul on his fourth missionary journey was in prison in Rome.

Epaphras, who is one of you and a servant of Christ Jesus, sends greetings. He is always wrestling in prayer for you, that you may stand firm in all the will of God, mature and fully assured. I vouch for him that he is working hard for you and for those at Laodicea and Hierapolis. Colossians ch.4 v12-13

Paul sends some final greetings. That you may stand firm, mature and indisputable. You are a servant of Jesus Christ, a believer in the faith and we will pray for you. 'Wrestling in prayer' means not a quick prayer, but a long, serious assurance for your safety.

The Church in Iconium

A city of Asia Minor, standing on the edge of the plateau. It was well watered, a productive and wealthy region. Its religion remained Phrygian and the worship of mother goddess with eunuch priests. Its fame and prestige grew greatly under Roman rule.

Paul and Barnabas on their first missionary journey went into the synagogue.

At Iconium Paul and Barnabas went as usual into the Jewish synagogue. There they spoke so effectively that a great number of Jews and Gentiles believed. Acts ch.14 v1

But the Jews who remained stirred up the Gentiles and poisoned their minds against what Paul and Barnabas were saying.

So Paul and Barnabas spent considerable time there, speaking boldly for the Lord, who confirmed the message of his grace by enabling them to do miraculous signs and wonders. Acts ch.14 v3

There was a difference of opinion. The Jews and Gentiles were going to ill-treat them and stone them for what they had done.

THE CHURCH IN LAODICEA

A city in the Roman province of Asia Minor. It was founded by the Seleucid Antiochus II and called after his wife, Laodice. Owing to its commercial centre under Roman rule and it was therefore an important centre of banking and exchange and the city was surrounded by fertile fields. It produced black fleeces from the sheep in the field. However, there was no permanent water supply, water had to be piped from hot springs some way off, but the pipes meant there will be only lukewarm water in the city.

Lying on the route of travellers and traders, Laodicea was reached by the gospel at an early date in about 30 AD.

I want you to know how much I am struggling for you and for those at Laodicea, and for all those who have not met me personally. My purpose is that they may be encouraged in heart and united in love ... Though I am absent to you in body, I am present with you in spirit and delight to see how orderly you are and how firm your faith in Christ is. Colossians ch.2 v1-2, v5

Paul was absent from Laodicea but present in spirit. He noted that how orderly your faith is.

I vouch for him (Epaphras) that he is working hard for you and for those at Laodicea ... Give my greetings to the brothers at Laodicea, and to Nympha and the church, her house. Colossians ch.4 v13, v15

He reminds the church that Epaphras was doing his best for you and for Nympha and her house which is being used for the Lord. It is a sacrifice when people come to the house, each neighbour knows that you are faithful to the Lord Jesus. Even Paul recognises that and she was a lady believer.

God said, "I know your deeds, that you are neither cold not hot. I wish you were either one or the other! So, because you are lukewarm - neither hot nor cold - I am about to spit you out of my mouth. You say, 'I am rich; I have acquired wealth and do not need a thing. But you do not realise that you are wretched, pitiful, poor, blind and naked ... So be earnest, and repent."
Revelation ch.3 v15-19

The church was in trouble; God reminded them of the water system and the prosperous trade coming in to the city. Because you are in the middle, neither hot not cold, he said that they were:

Wretched.

Pitiful.

Poor.

Blind.

Naked.

It is a horrible thing to say to a church. Jesus said, 'Repent and do the things that I instructed you to do.'

The Church in Lystra

An obscure town in south-central Asia Minor. Its remote position and the mountains all around may have suggested a defensive outlook. Lycaonia denoted that part of the territory which became a region of the province of Galatia. There was no suggestion of Roman order of justice as well as the usual Greeks and Jews.

But Paul and Barnabas on their first missionary journey.

But they found out about it and fled to the Lycaonian cites of Lystra and Derbe and to the surrounding country, where they continued to preach the good news. Acts ch.14 v6-7

They escaped from Iconium, because of the attention they received to ill-treat them. They preached the good news.

In Lystra there sat a man who was crippled in his feet, who was lame from birth and had never walked. Acts ch.14 v8

But there was a man who was crippled in his feet, he had never walked at all. He didn't understand walking. Most children maintain their balance and fell over as they struggled to walk. It takes a long time to walk.

Paul look directly at him, saw that he had faith to be healed and had called out, "Stand up on your feet!" At that the man jumped up and began to walk. Acts ch.14 v9-10

It was astounding. He jumped up and begun to walk properly.

Even with these words, they had difficulty keeping the crowd from sacrificing to them. Acts ch.14 v18

Then some Jews came for Antioch and Iconium and won the crowd over. It was a fickle crowd; they went from one thing to another. Praising God and stoning Paul.

They stoned Paul and dragged him outside the city, thinking that he was dead. But after the disciples had gathered round him, he got up and went back into the city. The next day he and Barnabas left for Derbe. Acts ch.14 v19-20

Stoning: The Mosaic law required that the prosecution witness had to cast the first stone, then if the victim still lived the spectators carried out the sentence and the body was suspended until sunset (see Deuteronomy ch.21 v22-23). It was carried out with the person in the middle, and couldn't get away. The person was on the ground and he managed to protect his face with his arms and kept very still.

Paul and Silas their second missionary journey.

The brothers at Lystra and Iconium spoke well of him (Timothy). Paul wanted to take him along on the journey. Acts ch.16 v2

He came to Derbe and then to Lystra where a disciple named Timothy lived.

On the fourth missionary journey when Paul was in prison and chained up in Rome, he wrote to Timothy:

You, however, know all about my teaching, my way of life, my purpose, faith, patience, love, endurance, persecutions, sufferings - what kinds of things happened to me in Antioch, Iconium and Lystra, the persecutions I endured. 2 Timothy ch.3 v10-11

He remarked that the stoning of Lystra had a marked effect on him. Timothy lived around there and he would understand what Paul had to suffer for the gospel of Jesus Christ to take the good news for the Jews, Gentiles and Romans.

THE CHURCH IN MEDES

Media was the ancient name south of the Caspian Sea and of the Zagros Mountains. The inhabitants were called Medes or Medians. The language is Aryan. Many Medes were given positions of responsibility and their custom and laws were combined with those of the Persians.

At The Feast of Pentecost there were some God-fearing Jews who travelled to Jerusalem either as visitors or as residents.

Parthians, Medes, Elamites … "We hear them declaring the wonders of God in our own tongues!" Amazed and perplexed, they asked one another, "What does this mean?" Acts ch.2 v9-12

Peter an apostle stood up and preached the gospel to the Jews.

Those who accepted his message were baptised, and about three thousand were added to their number that day. Acts ch.2 v41

Three thousand were added to number of believers. It was God making himself at one with the Jews who had come to worship him at the Feast of Pentecost. It was a marked changed from the church of God. How could they baptise all of them?

Each one from all around will go back to his home and rejoice in the news that the gospel had reached far and wide. This was the start of a new beginning.

THE CHURCH IN MILETUS

The great Ionian cites on the west coast of Asia Minor it was part of the Roman province. It flourished as a commercial centre, it established many colonies in the Black Sea area and also had contact with Egypt. There were several philosophers there. Milesian woollen goods were world famous. There were several changes and due to the silting up of its harbour from the Maeander River but it was declining commercially.

Paul was in his third missionary journey.

From Miletus, Paul sent to Ephesus for the elders of the church. When they arrived, he said to them: "You know how I lived the whole time I was with you ... For I have not hesitated to proclaim to you the whole will of God. Keep watch over yourselves and all the flock of which the holy Spirit has made you overseers. Be shepherds of the church of God." Acts ch.20 v17-18, v27-28

At the church in Miletus, Paul sent for the elders of the church at Ephesus to come to him and he instructed them about their duties. Even he, knowing what they had to do, he reminded them over an over again to look after their 'sheep'. Paul had a conscience that they might fall away and not hold up to the false teachers and prophets.

When he said this, he knelt down with all of them and prayed. They all wept as they embraced him and kissed him. What grieved them most as his statement that they would never see his face again. Acts ch.20 v36-38

He was adamant and convinced that he would never see them again. That was his last duty to remind the elders of the church in Ephesus.

Paul was on his fourth missionary journey as a prison in Rome, he remarked to Timothy:

"I left Trophimus sick in Miletus. Do your best to get here before winter." 2 Timothy ch.4 v20-21

He was in prison awaiting to go to the Emperor, but he still wrote to Timothy and he still remembered what will happen to Trophimus, who was indeed sick.

THE ABSENT CHURCH IN MYSIA

It was never a political place in the New Testament. It relied on the heavily forested hill country of either side of the main north road from Pergamum to Cyzicus on the Marmora Sea. Pergamum may be regarded as part of the district of Mysia.

Paul and Silas on their second missionary journey they tried to go to Galatia.

When they came to the border of Mysia, they tried to enter Bithynia, but the Spirit of Jesus would not allow them to. So they passed by Mysia and went down to Troas. Acts ch.16 v7-8

Troas was a Roman colony and an important seaport. Not passing through the district of Mysia, but going north to Macedonia. There is no mention of a church in Mysia, but there was a church in Troas adjacent to the Mediterranean Sea.

The Church in Pamphylia

A coastal region of south Asia Minor close to the Mediterranean Sea lying between Lycia and Cilicia. Pamphylia was part of Galatia. Across the sea there was Cyprus, a small island.

At the Feast of Pentecost when the Holy Spirit came on the believers, the devout Jews were there coming from Pamphylia as the apostle Peter gave a sermon explaining what had happened.

Then how is it that each of us hears them in his own native language? ... Phrygia and Pamphylia ... both Jews and converts to Judaism. Acts ch.2 v10-11

Paul and Barnabas on their first missionary journey.

From Paphos, Paul and his companions sailed to Perga in Pamphylia, where John left them to return to Jerusalem. Acts ch.13 v13

The route through Pamphylia on the coastal road made the journey to Jerusalem much easier than sailing by ship. We don't know why John Mark left them, he might have thought missionary life was not for him.

After going through Psidia, they came into Pamphylia, and when they had preached the word in Perga, they went down to Attalia. Acts ch.14 v24-25

They went up to the Euxine Sea and crossed to the Mediterranean Sea to Pamphyia and preached the word of God to all in Perga.

Paul and Silas on their second missionary journey.

Barnabas wanted to take John, also called Mark, with them, but Paul did not think it wise to take him, because he had deserted them in Pamphylia and had not continued with them in their work. They had such a sharp disagreement that they parted company. Barnabas took Mark and sailed for Cyprus. Acts ch.15 v38-39.

Barnabas was associated with John Mark; he was a cousin of Barnabas (see Colossians ch.4 v10). Barnabas and Mark sailed to Cyprus where Mark was known and understood.

Paul's fourth missionary journey, where he was to be taken to Rome as a prisoner.

When we had sailed across the open sea off the coast of Cilicia and Pamphylia, we landed at Myra and Lycia. There the centurion found an Alexandrian ship sailing for Italy and put us on board. Acts ch.27 v5-6

Cilicia and Pamphylia: adjoining provinces on the southern shore of Asia Minor. The centurion allowed Paul to meet with his friends so they might provide sustenance for his travels (see Acts ch.27 v3), so that there was a church in Pamphylia.

To go by ship to Rome it is a much easier way of getting there. Providing the weather is suitable. The only westerly wind would not allow a voyage towards the west to go round Greece (see Acts ch.27 v4).

The Absent Church in Parthia

Parthia, a district south of the Caspian Sea. On the east side it is close by the Media district. Their exclusive use of cavalry-bowmen made them a formidable enemy, as the Romans discovered to their cost. The Parthians were governed by a land-owning aristocracy, and controlled the lucrative trade with the Far East. There own religion was Iranian Mazdaism, but there was generally tolerant of other kinds of religion.

Paul didn't reach that far on his missionary travels, he followed the route round the Mediterranean Sea.

Now there were staying in Jerusalem God-fearing Jews from every nation under heaven ... Then how it is that each of us hears them in their own native language? Pathenian, Medes and Elamites. Acts ch.2 v5, v8-9

Again with Peter who explained the message of Jesus to the crowd of Jews there. The Jews would go back home and we don't know, it is not recorded in the Bible.

The Church in Patmos

A small island south-west of Ephesus it came under Asia Minor. It is about thirty-five miles south in the Mediterranean Sea. It probably served as a Roman penal settlement that the scenery was rocky because of the presence of a volcano. The island now belongs to Greece.

To this island the apostle John was banished.

I John, your brother and companion in the suffering and kingdom and patient endurance that are our in Jesus, was on the island of Patmos because the word of God and the testimony of Jesus. Revelation ch.1 v9

Believers were entering a time of persecution during the reign of the Emperor Vespasian. However, John wrote the book of Revelation there and could send it to help the churches. There must have been ships passing through and believers were on these boats.

Write on a scroll what you see and send it to the seven churches. Revelation ch.1 v11

He must have had a small place and he had a scroll and quill. An angel visited him and told him to write down his revelation of what might happen to the churches.

Which God gave him to show his servants what must soon take place. He made it known by sending his angel to his servant John, who testifies to everything he saw - that is, the word of God and testimony of Jesus Christ. Revelation ch.1 v1-2

He was a believer in the land of Patmos and he could help many people as a 'shepherd of the Lord's sheep'.

He was free to roam about the island but the place was indeed unstable or tottering due to the volcano. He was well versed in Scripture, a church leader well known to the seven churches he wrote to.

He passed the message on to a ship which would be present with believers. There must have been a church there. John is not the first to go there.

THE CHURCH IN PERGA

An ancient city in Pamphylia, well-sited in an extensive valley watered by the Cestrus River. It was the religious capital of Pamphylia whose temple stood on a nearby hill. Perga stands a little inland and was served by a river which flowed into the Mediterranean Sea.

On his first missionary journey Paul and Barnabas.

From Paphos, Paul and his companions sailed for Perga in Pamphylia. Acts ch.13 v13

They set out away from Cyprus and later they were going back to Antioch.

After going through Pisidia, they came into Pamphylia, and when they had preached the word in Perga, they went down to Attalia. Acts ch.14 v24

They preached the word and there was indeed a church in Perga.

THE CHURCH IN PERGAMUM

A city of the new Roman province of Asia Minor. It occupied a commanding position of the broad valley. It was bequeathed to the Romans who formed it into the province of Asia Minor. The temple of the imperial cult was built there in honour to Rome and Emperor Augustus, it was the official administrative capital of the province, as such it was the official religion and seat of imperial authority and justice in the region.

Pergamum was seen as the seat of the power of evil. Prisoners were brought to Pergamum as suspects and executed there after refusal to worship the Emperor.

God said, "To the angel of the church in Pergamum write ... where Satan has his throne. Yet you remain true to my name. You did not renounce your faith in me, even in the days of Antipas, my faithful witness, who was put to death in your city - where Satan lives. Nevertheless, I have a few things against you: You have people there who hold to the teaching of Balaam, who taught Balak to entice the Israelites to sin by eating food sacrificed to idols and by committing sexual immorality." Revelation ch.2 v12-14

Pergamum was evil, for example:

Satan has his throne.

Antipas was put to death in your city.

In the church there were many people.

Who sinned by eating food sacrificed to idols.

Who taught committing immorality was good.

Yet you remain true to God's name and did not renounce your faith at all.

The Church in Philadelphia

A city in the Roman province of Asia Minor and it was founded by Eumenes, King of Pergamum and named after his brother Attalus whose loyalty had been respected. It was situated near the upped end of the broad valley leading down through Sardis to the Mediterranean Sea near Smyrna. It was very fertile ground from which much of the commercial property was founded. The area was subject to frequent earthquakes and the city was remarkable for the number of its temples and religious festivals.

God said, "I know your deeds. See, I have placed before you an open door that no-one can shut. I know you have little strength, yet you have kept my word and have not denied my name ... Since you have kept my command to endure patiently, I will also keep you from the hour of trial that is going to come upon the whole world to test those who live on the earth." Revelation ch.3 v8, v10

The earthquakes, like little strength. The religious festivals, like the hour of trial kept the believers true to the name of the Lord.

THE CHURCH IN PONTUS

This coastal strip of north Asia Minor reaching from Bithynia in the west into the highlands of Armenia in the east. The region was politically a complex of Greek republics, temple estates and Iranian baronies.

When the Holy Spirit came on the believers at the Feast of Pentecost.

Now there were staying in Jerusalem God-fearing Jews from every nation under heaven ... Pontus and Asia. Acts ch.2 v5, v9

Even Pontus was filled with God-fearing Jews.

On their second missionary journey Paul and Silas.

There he met a man named Aquila, a native of Pontus, who had recently come from Italy with his wife Priscilla, because Claudius had ordered all the Jews to leave Rome. Paul went to see them, and because he was a tentmaker as they were, he stayed and worked with them. Acts ch.18 v2-3

Paul left Athens and went to Corinth and there he met a Jew named Aquilla. Because the Emperor Claudius (AD 41-54) had ordered all the Jews to leave Rome. The expulsion order for their continual tumults instigated by Chrestus (a common misspelling for Christ). If Chrestus does refer to Christ, the riots were obviously were about him, rather than led by him.

There was a church in Pontus and Paul being a tentmaker stayed with them.

Peter's letters.

Peter, an apostle of Jesus Christ, to God's elect, strangers in the world, scattered throughout Pontus ... who have been chosen according to the foreknowledge of God the Father, through the sanctifying work of the Spirit. 1 Peter ch.1 v1-2

Who have been chosen by God through the work of the Holy Spirit to make them holy or sacred. The believers are scattered throughout Asia Minor but came together in a church.

The Church in Phrygia

Prygia is close to Antioch. It is a tract of land centred on the Anatolian plateau. Most of the Phrygia was incorporated by the Romans into their province of Asia Minor. The eastern side was included in the new province of Galatia. The Romans were deeply impressed by the Phrygian cult of Cybele.

At the Feast of Pentecost, when the God-fearing Jews from each nation heard the sound in their own tongues as the Spirit enabled them, in their own native language.

Phrygia and Pamphylia … both Jews and converts to Judaism. Acts ch.2 v10-11

Those who accepted Peter's message were baptised, and about three thousand were added to their number that day. Acts ch.2 v41

Many Jews were converted and went back to their homes rejoicing in their faith.

Paul's second missionary journey.

Paul and his companions travelled throughout the region of Phrygia and

Galatia, having been kept by the Holy Spirit from preaching the word in the province of Asia. Acts ch.16 v6.

Paul, Silas and Timothy they had been preaching the word of the Lord. They went to Phrygia.

Paul's was on his third missionary journey:

After spending some time in Antioch, Paul set out from there and travelled from place to place throughout the region of Galatia and Phrygia, strengthening all the disciples. Acts ch.18 v23

Paul encouraged the believers to build up and stiffen, intensify what they would have to do as a church. It was amazing that they responded to Peter message during the Feast of Pentecost and they carried on doing the same things that they learnt.

The Church in Pisidia

A highland area in Asia Minor. The district lay at the western end of the Taurus range and was the home of lawless mountain tribes who defied the efforts of the Persian and their Hellenistic successors to subdue them. Sulpicius Quirinius finally imposed some sort of order and incorporated the region in the province of Galatia. The Roman peace brought prosperity to the district.

On his first missionary journey, Paul and Barnabas went there.

Paul and Barnabas travelled inland to Antioch of Pisidia. On the Sabbath they went to the synagogue for the services. After the usual readings from the books of Moses and the prophets, those in charge of the service sent them this message: "Brothers, if you have any word of encouragement for the people, come and give it." Acts ch.13 v14-15 (NLT)

The Jews and Gentiles were eager to hear the word of the Lord in the synagogue in Pisidia. They were ready to learn about the truths of God.

As Paul and Barnabas were leaving the synagogue, the people invited them to speak further about these things on the next Sabbath. When the congregation was dismissed, many of the Jews and devout converts to Judaism followed Paul and Barnabas, who talked with them and urged them to continue in the grace of God. Acts ch.13 v42-43

But the Jews were filled with jealousy and talked abusively against what Paul had been saying, they undermined the word of God. There was a distinct faction between the Jews and the believers. They talked and urged them to continue on with what they had learnt.

The word of the Lord spread through the whole region. Acts the ch.13 v49

The word spread rapidly as they believers went through the whole region explaining the difference that would make to them.

On his return, Paul and Barnabas went back to Pisidia.

After preaching the Good News in Derbe and making many disciples, Paul and Barnabas returned to Lystra, Iconium, and Antioch of Pisidia, where they strengthened the believers. They encouraged them to continue in the faith, reminding them that we must suffer many hardships to enter the Kingdom of God. Paul and Barnabas also appointed elders in every church. With prayer and fasting, they turned the elders over to the care of the Lord, in whom they had put their trust. Acts ch.14 v21-24 (NLT)

They encouraged them all to suffer hardships to continue in the faith of Jesus. They put faith in the elders of the church with prayer and fasting. They put their trust in the elders of the church and there was a strong church in Pisidia.

THE CHURCH IN SARDIS

A city in the Roman province of Asia Minor it was the capital of the ancient kingdom of Lydia. Its early prosperity came from the gold from the Pactolus, a stream which flowed through the city. The city was almost impregnable towering above the broad valley and nearly surrounded by precipitous cliffs of treacherous loose rock. It never regained under Roman rule what is had been in the past decades. The chief trade of the city was the making and dying of woollen garments.

God said, "I know your deeds, you have a reputation of being alive, but you are dead. Wake up! Strengthen what remains and is about to die, for I have not found your deeds complete in the sight of my God ... Yet you have a few people in Sardis who have not soiled their clothes. They will walk with me, dressed in white, for they are worthy." Revelation ch.3 v1-2, v4

Their gold under the Romans diminishes, so, 'strengthen what remains'. Your city was the making and selling garments and the church has come through with boldness and God feels it necessary to mention their clothes.

THE CHURCH IN SMYRNA

A city in the Roman province of Asia Minor. There was a Greek colony there, but it was capture by the Lydians and virtually ceased to exist until it was rebuilt by the Lysimachus. It grew to be one of the most prosperous cities in Asia Minor. It was the natural harbour for the ancient trade route through the Hermus valley. Smyrna was a faithful ally long before Rome had become the leading force. Under the Roman empire it was famous for its beauty and for the magnificent public buildings.

God said, "I know your afflictions and your poverty - yet you are rich! I know the slander of those who say they are Jews and are not, but are a synagogue of Satan. Do not be afraid of what you are about to suffer. I tell you, the devil will put some of you in prison to test you, and you will suffer persecution for ten days. Be faithful, even to the point of death, and I will give you the crown of life." Revelation ch.2 v9-10

It was exemplified in the courage with which the aged bishop Polycarp refused to recant and he was martyred in the city. The impressive and elegant buildings were there to hold the devil Satan and his fallen angels to do more evil against the church. It was going to be more suffering and in prison.

The Church in Tarsus

A city on the Cilician plain, by the River Cydnus and a few miles inland. The lower river was navigable and had a port. A main highway led to the Cilician Gates, the famous pass through the Taurus Mountains. Cicilia became a frontier region, this prompted the authorities to some reorganisation. In spite of the Roman influence with the land on the plain, Tarsus flourished.

Saul was converted on the Damascus road, so the Lord told Ananias in a vision to go and see Saul.

The Lord said, "Go over to Straight Street, to the house of Judas. When you get there, ask for a man from Tarsus named Saul. He is praying to me right now. I have shown him a vision of a man named Ananias coming in and laying hands on him so he can see again." Acts ch.9 v11-12 (NLT)

He is praying right now so Ananias would be there to support him and lay his hands upon him so that he might see again.

"Go! This man is my chosen instrument to carry my name before the Gentiles and their kings and before the people of Israel. I will show him how much he must suffer for my name." Acts ch.9 v15-16

Saul was called by the Lord and he was shown how much he would suffer for the name of Jesus. Before the Gentiles and their kings, it was a solemn promise that he would go to Rome to see the Emperor. Work with the Gentiles that God would include them into the church.

He debated with some Greek-speaking Jews, but they tried to murder him. When the believers heard about this, they took him down to Caesarea and sent him away to Tarsus, his hometown. Acts ch.9 v29-30 (NLT)

Saul when he was converted he went to Tarsus his hometown, so there was a church in Tarsus.

The Church in Thyatira

A city in the Roman province of Asia Minor. It occupied an important position connecting Hermus and Caicus valleys because of the low-lying places between them. It was a frontier garrison but it remained an important part in the road system, for it lay on the way from Pergamum to Laodicea. It was also an important centre of manufacture, dying, garment-making, pottery and brassware are all trades known to have existed there.

On the second missionary journey of Paul and Silas.

One of those listening was a woman named Lydia, a dealer in purple cloth from the city of Thyatira, who was a worshipper of God. The Lord opened her heart to respond to Paul's message. When she and her members of her household were baptised, she invited us to her home. "If you consider me as a believer in the Lord," she said, "come and stay at my house." Acts ch.16 v14-15

There was a woman there who let Paul come into her house, she was saved and her family.

God said, "I know you deeds, your love and faith, your service and perseverance, and that you are now doing more than you did at first. Nevertheless, I have this against you: You tolerate that woman Jezebel who calls herself by a prophetess. By her teaching she misleads the church into sexual immorality, the eating of food sacrificed to idols." Revelation ch.2 v19-20

Jezebel: The name is used here for a prominent woman in the church who undermined loyalty to God by promoting tolerance towards pagan practices (see 2 Kings ch.9 v22).

By her teaching, she was not allowed to teach being a woman, she was adamant that her sexual immorality and eating of food sacrificed to idols. This was there worst thing that she did, as a false prophetess.

The Church in Troas

Troas was founded near the site of the old city of Troy by the successors of Alexander the Great, and named after him Alexandria Troas. It was made a Roman colony by the Emperor Augustus and it was the main shipping route for travellers from Asia Minor to Macedonia.

On his second missionary journey Paul and Silas were not allowed to enter Galatia by the Holy Spirit.

So instead, they went on through Mysia to the seaport of Troas. Acts ch.16 v8 (NLT)

They went through to the seaport of Troas to go on a ship to Macedonia because the Mediterranean Sea was linked to the Euxine Sea.

On his third missionary journey Paul decided to go onto Macedonia.

These men went on ahead and waited for us at Troas. But we sailed from Philippi after the Feast of Unleavened Bread, and five days later joined the others at Troas, where we stayed seven days. Acts ch.20 v5-6

However, he was accompanied by seven men to go into Greece. This might have been because of a ship's schedule, but more probably he waited in order to meet with the brothers of the first day of the week to break bread.

On the first day of the week we came together to break bread. Paul spoke to the people and, because he intended to leave the next day, kept on talking until midnight. Acts ch.20 v7

A young man named Eutychus fell asleep and fell out of the window as Paul talked on. The floor where he fell was on the third storey up. But Paul went down, threw his arms around him and he was saved.

Now when I went to Troas to preach the gospel of Christ and found that the Lord had opened a door for me, I still had no peace of mind, because I did not find my brother Titus there. So I said good-bye to them and went on to Macedonia. 2 Corinthians ch.2 v12-13

When on his fourth missionary journey to Rome where he was imprisoned with a soldier round him with chains, so he remarked to Timothy:

When you come, bring the cloak that I left with Carpus at Troas, and my scrolls especially the parchments. 2 Timothy ch.4 v13

The scrolls were made of papyrus and the parchments were made of skin of animals. The later may have been copies of the Old Testament. But Paul left them there to help the believers.

GREECE

THE CHURCH IN ACHAIA

It was in Greece on the south coast of the gulf of Corinth. The area was administered with Macedonia at first, and the province was in the regular province and hence governed by a proconsul. Later, the province was connected with Corinth which is a much larger place.

Paul and Silas second missionary journey.

You know that the household of Stephanas were the first converts in Achaia, and they have devoted themselves to the service of the saints ... for they refreshed my spirit and yours also. Such men deserve recognition. 1 Corinthians ch.16 v15, v18

The first in Achaia to be saved as a believer. Stephanas was a good man and worthy of respect.

One night the Lord spoke to Paul in a vision: "Do not be afraid; keep on speaking, do not be silent. For I am with you, and no-one is going to attack and harm you, because I have many people in this city." So Paul stayed for a year and a half, teaching them the way of God. Acts ch.18 v9-11

Paul stayed with them for eighteen months because the Lord had spoken to him in a vision. There was a great potential in the city and Paul had to stay awhile teaching the believers. God will protect Paul and not let anyone attack and harm him.

While Gallio was proconsul of Achaia, the Jews made a united attack on Paul and brought him into court. Acts ch.18 v12

Eventually Paul had to go.

Paul's third missionary journey.

When Apollos wanted to go to Achaia, the brothers encouraged him and wrote to the disciples there to welcome him. On arriving, he was a great help to those who by grace had believed. For he vigorously refuted the Jews in public debate, proving from the Scriptures that Jesus was the Christ. Acts ch.18 v27-28

Apollos wanted to go to Achaia and the brothers supported and encouraged him because he was a great help to the people in Achaia. He vigorously refuted to Jews in the open, proving from the Scriptures that Jesus was the Christ the Son of God. The Jews didn't have anything to say about what the verses taught in the Old Testament.

Paul third missionary journey.

Paul decided to go to Jerusalem, passing through Macedonia and Achaia. Acts ch.19 v21

I am on my way to Jerusalem in the service of the saints there. For Macedonia and Achaia were pleased to make a contribution for the poor among the saints in Jerusalem. Romans ch.15 v25-26

He was encouraged to go to Achaia because he was a great help to the believers there. He planned to visit these places because the believers there were please to make a practical offering to the poor in Jerusalem.

So you became a model to all the believers in Macedonia and Achaia. 1 Thessalonians ch.1 v7

The Thessalonians did as Achaia had done. To provide funds for the destitute and poor believers back in Jerusalem.

The Church in Athens

Athens had a university there. It was also famous for its temples, statues and monuments. Though the Athens were religious and eager to discuss religion, their spiritual level was poor. Their love of human sacrifices in the gladiatorial games was appalling.

Paul was in Athens on his second missionary journey.

While Paul was waiting for them (Silas and Timothy) in Athens, he was greatly distressed to see that the city was full of idols. So he reasoned in the synagogue with the Jews and God-fearing Greeks, as well as in the market-place day by day with those who happened to be there. Acts ch.17 v16-17

A group of philosophers argued with him. All the Athenians and the foreigners who lived there spent all their time doing nothing but debating the latest ideas.

Then they took him and brought him to a meeting of the Areopagus, where they said to him, "May we know what this new teaching is that you are presenting." Acts ch.17 v19

When they heard him talking him talking about 'raising the dead' some of them sneered, but others said, "We want to hear you again on this subject."

A few men became followers of Paul and believed. Among them was Dionysius, a member of the Areopagus, also a woman named Damaris, and a number of others. Acts ch.17 v34

Only a few became believers.

So when we could stand it no longer, we thought it best to be left by ourselves in Athens. 1 Thessalonians ch.3 v1

It was a disappointment for Paul, since the Athens were eager to discuss a new religion. But the Greeks didn't respond to Jesus being resurrected, so they couldn't believe in Jesus and what he had achieved.

All of Athens, a marvellous city with a lot of idols, but only a few believed and Paul went into the Areopagus to tell them of Jesus, the Messiah. They considered themselves custodians of teaching that introduced new religious and foreign gods, but they had traditions that wouldn't face that Jesus had been resurrected.

THE CHURCH IN BEREA

A city of southern Macedonia and it was evidently a prosperous centre with a Jewish colony.

On his second missionary journey Paul and Silas went to see the Bereans.

Now the Bereans were of more noble character than the Thessalonians, for they received the message with great eagerness and examined the Scriptures every day to see if what Paul said was true. Many of the Jews believed, as did also a number of prominent Greek women and many Greek men. Acts ch.17 v11-12

There was a lot of work to do, building up the church. The Jews at Thessalonica caught up with them there, they had been jealous of what Paul had been doing in the synagogue in Thessalonica.

The brothers immediately sent to Paul to the coast, but Silas and Timothy stayed at Berea. Acts ch.17 v14

The third missionary journey Paul decided to go through Macedonia.

He was accompanied by Sopater son of Pyrrhus from Berea. Acts ch.20 v4

He was with Sopater from Berea. One of the many people of the church there, but several other six people went with him. We don't know what Sopater did in the Bible, but he was the first name in the book of Acts.

The Church in Cenchrea

A town near Corinth which served as an outpost, managing its transport. There is a port located about six miles east of Corinth on the Saronic Gulf.

Paul on his third missionary journey.

Before he sailed (to Ephesus), he had his hair cut off at Cenchrea because of a vow he had taken. Acts ch.18 v18

Paul had his hair cut off because he had taken a vow. Different vows were frequently taken to express thanks for deliverance from grave dangers. Not necessarily a Nazarite vow (see Numbers ch.6 v1-21).

Paul on his fourth missionary journey to Rome.

I commend to you our sister Phoebe, a servant of the church in Cenchrea. I ask you to receive her in the Lord in a way of the saints and to give her any help she may need from you, for she has been a great help to many people, including me. Romans ch.16 v1-2

Probably the carrier of the letter to Rome. It was a dangerous and perilous journey and it was a woman who travelled there. There was no postal service each time one had a letter it was important that they be carried (see

2 Corinthians ch.11 v26-27). This was what it was like for her:

> She would have been constantly on the move.
>
> She would be in danger from rivers.
>
> She must go with bandits around her.
>
> She has to go in danger form Gentiles who might molest her.
>
> She is in danger from the city she speaks a different language.
>
> She is in danger from out in the countryside.
>
> She is in danger from the sea on her own.
>
> She is in danger from false brothers who she didn't know.

Paul said, 'Give her any help that she needed'. For she has been a great help to many people, including me. She had a duty to carry letters, and she did it more than once. I believe she wasn't married otherwise her husband would be there with her.

THE CHURCH IN CORINTH

A chief city of Greece that managed a flourishing centre of trade as well as for industry, this was taken across the land rather than round the stormy seas. It was a crossroads for travellers and traders and it had two harbours. The city is dominated by a steep flat-topped rock which in turn contained the temple of Aphrodite, the goddess of love, whose service gave rise to the city's immorality. At one time 1,000 sacred prostitutes served her temple.

It is small wonder that the Corinthian church was plagued with numerous problems.

Paul and Silas second missionary journey.

Paul left Athens and went to Corinth ... Every Sabbath he reasoned in the synagogue, trying to persuade Jews and Greeks. Acts ch.18 v1, v4

Each Sabbath on the Saturday he went into the synagogue. But the opposition was enormous. The Jews and Greeks preferred to go along with what they had been doing. They didn't want to turn and follow Jesus.

But when the Jews opposed Paul and became abusive, he shook out his clothes in protest and said to them, "Your blood be on your own heads! I am clear of my responsibility. From now on I will go to the Gentiles." Acts ch.18 v6

Even the Jews were caught up with the immorality, not particularly the Greeks. He reasoned that his duty was finished, he would go to the Greeks. He was making a distinction between the Jews and the Greeks. That is why they had later a Conference in Jerusalem (see Acts ch.15 v1-35).

Crispus, the synagogue ruler, and his entire household believed in the Lord; and many of the Corinthians who heard him believed and were baptised. Acts ch.18 v8

The synagogue ruler believed and his house that was the start of the work at Corinth. It would make a considerable difference to the work of the synagogue, the ruler might have to stand down with all the prostitution going on, even affecting the Jews.

To the church of God in Corinth, to those sanctified in Christ Jesus and called to be holy. 1 Corinthians ch.1 v2

It would be a holy place to separate themselves off, they would be questioned and noticed. God doesn't like the immoral temple at Corinth, he really hates it.

Later, Corinth was a riotous place and several members of the church had serious problems (See in 1 and 2 Corinthians), for example:

The divisions separating them.

The laxity in church discipline.

Lawsuits before non-Christian judges.

The sexual immorality.

The instruction on marriage.

The instruction of proper worship.

The work on spiritual gifts.

The instruction of the resurrection.

Paul said: "So, if you think you are standing firm, be careful that you don't fall! No temptation has seized you except from what is common to man. And God is faithful; he will not let you be tempted beyond what you can bear. But when you are tempted, he will also provide a way out so that you can stand up under it" 1 Corinthians ch.10 v12-13

Paul said, 'If you are standing fixed on solid ground, God will not let you fall'. But he has provided a way so you can stand up under it (see 1 John ch.1 v8-10).

The Church in Greece

The republics were the Black Sea, Sicily and South Italy and as far west as Spain. Greece was never a political entity. Under Roman rule they were systematically broken up into Greek republics. They provided not only education but brilliant entertainment and a wide range of health and welfare services. It was membership of the Greek language that marked a man as civilised, all the others were barbarians.

Paul and Silas were on their second missionary journey.

That night Paul had a vision: A man from Macedonia in northern Greece was standing there, pleading with him, "Come over to Macedonia and help us!" So we decided to leave for Macedonia at once, having concluded that God was calling us to preach the Good News there. Acts ch.16 v9-10 (NLT)

He concluded that God had called us to Greece to preach the gospel to them. They were among the first converts in Achaia, along with the few individuals in Athens who had believed a short time earlier (see Acts ch.17 v34).

You know that Stephanas and his household were the first of the harvest of believers in Greece, and they are spending their lives in service to God's people. I urge you, dear brothers and sisters, to submit to them and others like them who serve with such devotion. I am very glad that Stephanas, Fortunatus, and Achaicus have come here. They have been providing the help you weren't here to give me. They have been a wonderful encouragement to me, as they have been to you. You must show your appreciation to all who serve so well. 1 Corinthians ch.16 v15-16 (NLT)

They have been providing the help and encouragement to Paul. It was a new ground for him to preach in Greece, nobody had ever done it before.

Paul on his third missionary journey.

He set out for Macedonia. He travelled through that area, speaking many words to encouragement to the people, and finally arrived in Greece, where he stayed three months. Acts ch.20 v1-2

The two Roman provinces (Macedonia and Achaia) into which Greece was divided (see Acts ch.19 v21 and Romans ch.15 v26).

As a result, you have become an example to all the believers in Greece—throughout both Macedonia and Achaia. 1 Thessalonians ch.1 v7 (NLT)

He stayed for three months, helped the churches by giving words of encouragement.

The Church in Macedonia

A splendid area centred on the plains of the gulf of Thessalonica, flowing down the great river valley from the Balkan Mountains. It was famous for timber and precious metal. Macedonia was four federations under the Romans, they were subsequently grouped under the Roman Provincial Control and were heavily guarded against the northern frontier. The proconsul sat at Thessalonica, while the assembly of the Greek states met at Berea. There were no Jews and no synagogue.

Paul on his third missionary journey.

I planned to visit you first so that you might benefit twice. I planned to visit you on my way to Macedonia and to come back to you from Macedonia, and then to have you send me on my way to Judea. 2 Corinthians ch.1 v15-16

He was anxious to aid the churches in Macedonia, perhaps due to the vision he had in Galatia. There were many churches in Macedonia, like Philippi and Thessalonica. It was the pathway going round the Mediterranean Sea and the Euxine Sea to go to Italy, without taking a ship passing by Crete.

Paul sent two of his helpers, Timothy and Erastus, to Macedonia while he stayed in the province of Asia a little longer. Acts ch.19 v22

He stayed for a while longer in Macedonia with two of his helpers.

When we came into Macedonia, this body of ours had no rest, but we were harassed at every turn - conflicts on the outside, fears within. But God, who comforts the downcast, comforted us by the coming of Titus. 2 Corinthians ch.7 v5-6

The coming of Titus gave Paul some extra help.

When I was with you and needed something, I was not a burden to anyone, for the brothers who had come from Macedonia supplied what I needed. I have kept myself from being a burden to you in any way, and will continue to do so. 2 Corinthians ch.11 v9

Paul had difficulties in Macedonia but the coming of Titus comforted him and he worked hard to prevent them from being a burden to anyone.

For Macedonia and Achaia were pleased to make a contribution for the poor among the saints in Jerusalem. Romans ch.15 v26

The Macedonian churches provided gifts for the poor in Jerusalem. They understood from Greece to Israel it is a long, hard journey over seas. It was kind of them to do it. Like the churches in England to help the poor in Africa.

We want you to know about the grace that God has given the Macedonia churches. Out of the most severe trial, their overflowing joy and their extreme poverty welled up in rich generosity. For I testify that they gave as much as they were able, and even beyond there ability. Entirely on their own, they urgently pleaded with us for the privilege of sharing in this service to the saints. 2 Corinthians ch.8 v1-4

They would know that under their most severe trial they have given much money even beyond what they were used to, their ability to give. Entirely on their own they gave what they had to the service of the saints.

The Church in Nicopolis

It is on the west coast of Greece. A town built as the capital of Epirus by Emperor Augustus on a peninsular of the Ambraciot Gulf. It was a Roman colony and derived some of its importance from the Actian games, also by Augustus.

I am as I send Artemas or Tychicus to you, do your best to come to me at Nicopolis, for I have decided to the winter there. Titus ch.3 v12

We are not sure if Paul had a church in Nicopolis, but he stayed over there for the winter. Paul could either have gone to Achaia or Corinth, but he stayed there with the believers.

The Church in Philippi

The city of Philippi was named after Philip II of Macedon. Father of Alexander the Great took it over from the Thasians and he enlarged the settlement and fortified it to defend his territory. At this time the gold-mining industry was developed and expanded. After the Romans arrived Philippi became unrecognised, they divided it up into four parts for administrative purposes. They had a theatre, the forum and the baths, it was a prosperous town. They prided themselves on being Roman, dressed like Romans and often spoke Latin. Many of the retired military men had been given land and who in turn served as a military presence, which may explain why there were not many Jews and no synagogue.

From there we travelled to Philippi, a Roman colony and the leading city of that district of Macedonia. Acts ch.16 v12

Paul and Silas on their second missionary journey.

There were no Jews, so Paul and Silas went down to the river where they expected to find a place of prayer along the banks of the Gangites River. It was customarily for such places to be outdoors near running water.

On the Sabbath we went outside the city gate to the river, where we expected to find a place of prayer. We sat down and began to speak to the women who had gathered there. One of those listening was a woman named Lydia. Acts ch.16 v13-14.

Paul reasoned with Lydia who was a dealer in purple cloth from the city in Thyatira. She was open to him and she listened well. She was used to people talking to her, a dealer, so Paul didn't have a problem with all the ladies present.

Once when we were going to the place of prayer, we were met by a slave girl who had a spirit by which she predicted the future. She earned a great deal of money for her owners by fortune-telling. Act ch.16 v16

Paul became so troubled that he turned round and cast out the spirit. The owners seized Paul and Silas and dragged them into the market place to face the authorities. The crowd joined in the attack on them and the magistrates ordered them to be stripped and beaten and they were thrown into prison.

Suddenly in the jail there was an earthquake and the prison doors were opened. The jailer was frightened thinking that the prisoners were gone.

Jailer: if the prisoner escaped, the life of the jailer was demanded in his place. To take his own life he would shorten the shame and distress that would be caused by his family.

They (Paul and Silas) replied, "Believe in the Lord Jesus, and you will be saved - you and your household." Then they spoke the word of the Lord to him and to all the others in his house ... Because he had come to believe in God - he and his whole family. Acts ch.16 v31-32, v34

Paul and Silas said, 'Believe in the Lord Jesus and you will be saved and even your family with you'. He spoke more words to them and to the others in his house and they believed in Jesus.

Paul said, "They beat us publicly without a trial, even though we are Roman citizens, and threw us into prison" ... They (the magistrates) came to appease them and escorted them from the prison, requesting them to leave the city. Acts ch.16 v37, v39

The magistrates came to satisfy them and helped them out of the city so that they could go on their way. To avoid the offence that was illegal in what they did.

Roman citizens: public beating for a Roman citizen would have been illegal, let alone beating without a trial. Paul and Silas were not asking for an escort out of the city, as much as they were establishing their innocence for the sake of the church in Philippi and its future.

After Paul and Silas came out of the prison, they went to Lydia's house, where they met with the brothers and encouraged them. Then they left. Acts ch.16 v40

Paul decided he didn't want to go, but he went to Lydia's house where they went to encouraged them in what they were doing. To satisfy them in Philippi.

Paul on his third missionary journey.

Moreover, as you Philippians know, in the early days of your acquaintance with the gospel, when I set out from Macedonia, not one church shared with me in the matter of giving and receiving, except you only; for even when I was in Thessalonica, you sent me aid again and again when I was in need. Philippians ch.4 v14-16

The Philippians shared what they had to get Paul into Greece. It was only the church doing it, nobody else. They gave me provisions time after time, they carried on doing it for several months or even years. While Paul was in need.

Paul on his fourth missionary journey.

To all the saints in Christ Jesus at Philippi, together with the overseers and deacons: grace and peace to you from God our Father and the Lord Jesus Christ. Philippians ch.1 v1-2

He was chained up in Rome with a guard close by (see Acts ch.28 v16), he remarked there was a growing church in Philippi. 'Grace and peace to you', there was opposition from the Jews (see Philippians ch.3 v1-3, v18-19)

We had previously suffered and been insulted in Philippi, as you know, but with the help of our God we dared to tell you his gospel in spite of strong opposition. 1 Thessalonians ch.2 v1-2

Paul had previously suffered and being insulted in Philippi but dared explain his gospel in spite of strong opposition.

As you Philippians know, in the early days of your acquaintance with the gospel, when I set out from Macedonia, not one church shared with me in the matter of giving and receiving, except you only; for even when I was in Thessalonica, you sent me aid again and again when I was in need. Philippians ch.4 v15-16

They presented Paul with money when he was in need going though Greece. Nobody thought that the missionary would need help but the church in Philippi new best.

THE CHURCH IN THESSALONICA

Thessalonica was a bustling seaport city at the head of the Thermaic Gulf. It became an important communication and trade centre, located at the junction of the great Egnatian Way and the road leading north to the Danube. Its population is about 200,000 making it the largest city in Macedonia. Her position under the Romans was assured.

Paul on his second missionary journey came with Silas to Thessalonica.

Where there was a Jewish synagogue. As his custom was, Paul went in to the synagogue, and on three Sabbath days he reasoned with them from the Scriptures, explaining and proving the Christ had to suffer and rise from the dead. Acts ch.17 v1-3

Paul went into the synagogue and one three days logically and well-thought-out with them about Jesus. He explained and proved that Jesus was the Messiah and had to suffer and die for us all.

Some of the Jews were persuaded and joined Paul and Silas, as did a large number of God-fearing Greeks and not a few prominent women. Acts ch.17 v4

Many of the Jews and Greeks were persuaded and joined Paul and Silas. It is surprising that the Thessalonicas were better prepared than the Athenians, where Paul said the same gospel.

But the Jews were jealous, so they rounded up some bad characters from the market-place, formed a mob and started a riot in that city, Acts ch.17 v5

The Jews were envious and bore a grudge against Paul. So they rounded up some bad characters in the market-place and started an uprising and rebellion in that city.

On his third missionary journey, Paul went to Macedonia.

He was accompanied by ... Aristarchus and Secundus from Thessalonica. Acts ch.20 v4

Seven people went with him and these men went on ahead and waited for him at Troas. It was the Feast of Unleavened Bread in Philippi.

Paul's fourth missionary journey.

Aristarchus, a Macedonian from Thessalonica, was with us. Acts ch.27 v2

He sails as a prisoner to Rome following what he had been doing in the temple at Jerusalem and Aristarchus was with Paul.

Aristarchus: with the riot in Ephesus and soon the whole city was in an uproar, so the people seized Gaius and Aristarchus, Paul's travelling companions (see Acts ch.19 v29). My fellow prisoner Aristarchus sends you his greetings, as does Mark, the cousin of Barnabas (see Colossians ch.4 v10). So do Mark, Aristarchus, Demas and Luke, my fellow-workers (see Philemon ch.1 v24). This was a dangerous journey until Paul met with the Nero the Emperor. Aristarchus was there throughout his journey and Nero would sacrifice the Christians to get rid of them. Aristarchus was also a prisoner with Paul.

Paul was later in prison in Rome.

The former preach Christ out of selfish ambition, not sincerely, supposing that they can stir up trouble for me while I am in chains. But what does it matter? Philippians ch.1 v17-18

What does it matter if Jesus is preached and taught? Paul was there in chains but his thought was with the churches.

Now about brotherly love we do not need to write to you, for you yourselves have been taught by God to love each other. And in fact, you do love all the brothers throughout Macedonia. Yet we urge you, brothers, do so more and more. 1 Thessalonians ch.4 v9-10

It was an expression of love between them.

Paul's had left Thessalonica abruptly after a brief stay. His purpose was to encourage these two letters to give the new converts in their trials, to give instructions about holy living and not to neglect daily work. To give assurance concerning the future and what it means (see 1 and 2 Thessalonians).

CRETE

THE CHURCH IN CRETE

The fourth largest island in the Mediterranean Sea, Crete lies directly south of the Aegean Sea. A mainly mountainous island, but Crete had descended to a lower moral level, the dishonesty, gluttony and laziness of its inhabitants (see Titus ch.1 v12).

When the Holy Spirit came upon the believers and they all spoke in tongues at the Feast of Pentecost.

Cretans and Arabs - "We hear them declaring the wonders of God in our own tongues!" Amazed and perplexed, they asked one another, "What does this mean?" Acts ch.2 v11-12

Paul's fourth missionary journey.

Since the harbour was unsuitable to winter in, the majority decided that we should sail on, hoping to reach Phoenix and winter there. This was a harbour in Crete, facing both south-west and north-west. Acts ch.27 v12

While he was going to meet the Emperor, as a prisoner. He left Caesarea by boat and they weighed anchor and sailed along the shore of Crete.

Men, you should have taken my advice not to sail from Crete; then you would have spared yourselves this damage and loss. Acts ch.27 v21

When the hurricane force swept down and the ship was in danger from the waves and storms. The ship was spared by God and ran aground in Malta, but the rest of the boat was smashed to pieces.

Paul on his fifth missionary journey went to Crete.

Following Paul's release from his Roman imprisonment (see Acts ch.28 v30), he and Titus worked in Crete.

There are a number of points that he was released from his imprisonment: Acts stopped abruptly at this time.

> Paul wrote to churches expecting to visit them there and he was expecting a release (see Philippians ch.2 v24 and Philemon ch.1 v22).

> Paul's letters do not fit in with the historical account in Acts (see Titus).

The reason I left you in Crete was that you might strengthen out what was left unfinished and appoint elders in every town, as I directed you. Titus ch.1 v5

After his release from Paul's imprisonment in Rome. There was a many churches in Crete, so Paul indicated to Titus that he must consolidate the believers and allow them to come together. This was the job of elders in the churches. Titus was obviously a capable and resourceful leader and he would appoint elders in every town.

ITALY

THE ABSENT CHURCH IN ILLYRICUM

The name of a large mountainous region on the east of the Adriatic. Its name was derived from that of the first tribes within it boundaries that the Greeks came across. Its inhabitants spoke dialects which were probably the modern Albanian. When it was divided up by the Romans into two separate areas.

Paul on his third missionary journey.

So from Jerusalem all the way round to Illyricum, I have fully proclaimed the gospel of Christ. It has always been my ambition to preach the gospel where Christ was not known, so that I would not be building on someone else's foundation. Romans ch.15 v19-20

Paul said, writing to the Romans, this was the limit of his missionary journeys. It has always been my ambition to preach Jesus where God's word has not been reached. This was remarkable, Paul hardships were known about (see 2 Corinthians ch.11 v23-28).

There might have been a church there, but the Scriptures are silent about it.

This is why I have often been hindered from coming to you (in Rome). Romans ch.15 v22

There was no believers or churches there in the Bible. But Paul had believed that his work was done and he widely proclaimed the message of Jesus. That coming to Jesus required faith and deeds (see James ch.2 v14-26).

The Church in Italy

Even before the time of Jesus many Jews had gone to Italy.

Paul on his forth missionary journey.

When it was decided that we would sail for Italy, Paul and some other prisoners were handed over to a centurion named Julius, who belonged to the Imperial Regiment. Acts ch.27 v1

He not a criminal and not a politically dangerous rival, so he could live by himself, but a guard had to remain with him, perhaps chained to him. If Paul escaped, the guard would have to pay with his life (see Acts ch.28 v16).

For two whole years Paul stayed their in his own rented house and welcomed all who came to see him. Boldly and without hindrance he preached the kingdom of God and taught about the Lord Jesus Christ. Acts ch.28 v30-31

There was a church in Italy and he preached and taught the word of God. Even the guard new about it and the word passed between the soldiers.

Greet all your leaders and all God's people. Those from Italy send you their greetings. Hebrews ch.13 v24

He wrote several letters like 1 and 2 Timothy, and then passed them on to Timothy and the believers. He welcomed all God's people, Jews and Gentiles alike.

The Church in Puteoli

It was near Naples; a Samian colony it was dominated by the Romans. Rapidly becoming an important arsenal and trading port. Rome's eastern traffic, notably the Egyptian grain, passed though Puteoli.

Paul on his fourth missionary journey.

The next day the south wind came up, and on the following day we reached Puteoli. There we found some brothers who invited us to spend a week with them. And so we came to Rome. Acts ch.28 v13-14

Paul as a prisoner being taken to the Emperor Nero. The centurion, Julius had business to attend to and then stayed away. Paul found some brothers who invited us to spend a week with them, it was a delight for his travels including a stay in Malta over three months (see Acts ch.28 v10-11).

There was a church in Puteoli.

THE CHURCH IN ROME

In terms of political importance, position and sheer magnificence, the city of the empire was Rome the capital. Founded traditionally on its seven hills east of the Tiber River and was originally a meeting place. Rome had several impressive public buildings, aqueducts, baths and theatres. The most prominent feature was the Capitoline Hill with temples to Jupiter and Juno.

Rome had reason for pride in its buildings and shame for the urban social problems. As the seat of the Senate and through the Emperors to control all of the land.

Visitors of Rome both Jews and converts to Judaism ... we hear them declaring the wonders of God in our own tongues. Acts ch.2 v10-11

When the Holy Spirit came on the Feast of Pentecost, Rome was there. Even the journey by ship would have taken some while and cost a lot of money.

Paul and Silas on their second missionary journey.

There he met a Jew named Aquila, a native of Pontus, who had recently come from Italy with his wife Priscilla, because Claudius had ordered all the Jews to leave Rome. Paul went to see them, and because he was a tentmaker as they were, he stayed and worked with them. Acts ch.18 v2-3

Paul being a tent-maker joined up with Aquila and Priscilla. He would have been doing this trade while he was young. It was the Jewish custom to provide manual training for sons, whether rich or poor.

Paul on his third missionary journey, he remarked,

Paul decided to go to Jerusalem, passing through Macedonia and Achaia (Greece). "After I have been there," he said, "I must visit Rome also." Acts ch.19 v21

Paul wanted to speak to the masses of crowds in Rome.

I urge you, brothers, to watch out for those who cause divisions and put obstacles in your way that are contrary to the teaching you have learned. Keep away from them. Romans ch.16 v17

Paul wrote the book of Romans to look out for those who cause divisions among you. Like false teachers and prophets. He said, "Keep away from them." To avoid being seduced by the evil persons.

You also are among those who have been called to belong to Jesus Christ. To all who are at Rome who are loved by God and called to be saints. Romans ch.1 v6-7

He was going there to meet with the believers and share the gospel in the market place.

I am bound both the Greeks and non-Greeks, both to the wise and foolish. that is why I am so eager to preach the gospel also to you who are at Rome. Romans ch.1 v14-15

He waited and preached to the Greeks and Barbarians, both to the wise and foolish.

Barbarians: a word that probably imitated the unintelligent sound of their languages to Greek ears. Barbarian does mean they were savages and in some ways they could neither read not write, like in England.

Paul on his fourth missionary journey.

The following night the Lord stood near Paul and said, "Take courage! As you have testified about me in Jerusalem, so you must also testify in Rome." Acts ch.23 v11

The Lord stood by Paul, in times of crisis and need for strength he was given help with the Jewish plot to kill Paul. The Lord said, 'As you have testified about me, take courage you must also testify about me in Rome'. To preach to the Emperor, right at the top of the civil authorities. To go to the Emperor the believers thought that they could separate themselves off from the Jews. To have a new start.

The brothers (in Rome) there had heard that we were coming, and they travelled as far as the Forum of Appius and the Three Taverns to meet us. At the sight of these men Paul thanked God and was encouraged. Acts ch.28 v15

The church was based in Rome and had Jews and Gentiles together. It must have comforted Paul to see how they responded to him.

They (in Rome) replied, "We have not received any letters from Judea concerning you, and none of the brothers who have come from here has reported or said anything bad about you. But we want to hear what your views are, for we know that people everywhere are talking against this sect ...

From morning to evening he explained and declared to them the kingdom of God and tried to convince them about Jesus from the Law of Moses and from the Prophets. Some were convinced by what he said, but others would not believe. Acts ch.28 v21-24

When the got to Rome, the friends there had not heard anything about Paul. The places were so far away and it would be difficult to send letters back and forth. so the Jews in Jerusalem would take it that Paul had been killed.

What Would the Church Be Doing?

The Way of New Life

There was some Jewish Christians who believed and held that a number of ceremonial practices on the Old Testament were still binding on the church.   Following Paul's on his first and second missionary journey campaign in Galatia.   They insisted on trying to make the Gentiles obey certain rites.

You can see what Paul made on his letter to the Galatians:

There is neither Jew nor Greek, slave or free, male nor female, for you all one in Christ Jesus. If you belong to Christ. Galatians ch.3 v28

You are all one if you belong to Jesus. There is no difference between us whatever we are.

Since we live by the Spirit, let us keep in step with the Spirit.   Let us not become conceited, provoking and envying each other. Galatians ch.5 v25-26

Don't become conceited thinking that you are better than the other person.

The one who sows to please his sinful nature, from that nature will reap destruction; the one who sows to please the Spirit, from the Spirit will reap eternal life. Galatians ch.6 v8

From the Holy Spirit you could exercise a right conscience, look to the other person as a believer. We are all saved by accepting Jesus life, his death, his burial and his resurrection. Nothing can come between us and certainly not Jewish practices or rites.

Now that faith has come, we are no longer under the supervision of the law. Galatians ch.3 v25

It is a marked change from the Jewish traditions in the Old Testament, to a new beginning after Jesus was crucified and was dead.

At that moment, the curtain of the temple was torn in two from top to bottom. The earth shook and the rocks split. Matthew ch.27 v51

The curtain of the temple 'was torn in two', meaning that God would welcome all who came to him with repentance from the old way of life that we lived and accepting Jesus as Lord and Saviour of our lives.

No Splits in the Church

There were no divisions in the church, not even in Corinth. After the Bible was written, man based in his tradition he engineered all of the splits and divisions. Now we have hundreds more churches, all who had the 'right way' to go. Many modern churches don't seem to have grasped that.

It is 'Christ unity' that binds all of us together.

Do you not think that when Jesus came back he would take his followers to be with himself? There is no distinction between believers. It is disappointing that in the towns there are lots of Christians who don't seem to have understood that we are all one, regardless of the church we happen to attend.

It is important that we join with all other believers to let the world know that we are saved. Not to separate us from each other.

Jesus said, "May they be brought to complete unity to let the world know that you sent me and have loved them even as you have loved me." John ch.17 v23

Unity is what counts and it is based on love.

The Pharisees broke their law for traditions based on the past (see Matthew ch.15 v3-6). This is clearly not what Jesus taught. He maintained that the Old and New Testaments should be regarded as true and certain.

They worship me in vain; their teachings are but rules taught by men. Matthew ch.15 v9

Only men conscripted the rules or traditions. They were not there in the Old and New Testament.

All Scripture is God-breathed and is useful for teaching, rebuking, correcting and training in righteousness, so that the man of God may be thoroughly equipped for every good work. 2 Timothy ch.3 v16-17

All scripture is God-breathed and man's rules and traditions are not.

Then they understood that he was not telling them to guard against the yeast used in bread, but against the teaching of the Pharisees and Sadducees. Matthew ch.16 v12

The yeast is telling them to be careful from the Jewish teachers to have a tradition that involves them departing from God's word. The yeast is a potent product that goes through the bread making all of it to be fit for baking. It is the same is true today. The yeast goes through the church and everybody is affected by it, even the elders and leaders of the church. Everybody is confined by it and the God's word would be passed over and removed.

In the last book of the Bible:

I warn everyone who hears the words of the prophecy of this book: If anyone adds anything to them, God will add to him the plagues described in this book. And if anyone takes words away from this book of prophecy, God will take away from him his share in the tree of life and in the holy city, which are described in this book. Revelation v22 v18-19

This is a solemn promise that if anyone takes or adds this prophecy God would do so likewise. Prophecy lasts for over many years and God's word is sure to come true, regardless of man's human tradition.

No splits or divisions in the church.

A New Priesthood

In the Old Testament we have priests to get the Israelites ready to meet God in his temple.

The priests are to keep my requirement so that they do not become guilty and die for treating them with contempt. I am the Lord, who makes them holy. Leviticus ch.22 v9

In the Tent of Meeting and the two temples, it was a solemn occasion and nobody could enter the Holy Place where the ark was and God's incense was placed by the priests.

Once when Zechariah's division was on duty and he was serving as priest before God; he was chosen by lot, according to the custom of the priesthood, to go into the temple of the Lord and burn incense. Luke ch.1 v8-9 (see Hebrews ch.9 v1-10).

Only once a year a priest entered and made supplications for the sins of the Israelites.

Day after day every priest stands and performs his religious duties; again and again he offers the same sacrifices, which can never take away sins. Hebrews ch.10 v11

The rules must be kept so that there is a priest for mankind to meet God; he is a mediator between mankind and God. After Jesus was killed, he offered his body once for all to let people come to God; he sacrificed himself. Now there is no need for any of the priests. As believers, you can come to God willingly.

As Peter said,

Are being built into a spiritual house to be a holy priesthood, offering spiritual sacrifices acceptable to God through Jesus Christ ... But you are a chosen people, a royal priesthood, a holy nation, a people belonging to God, that you may declare the praises of him who called you of darkness into his wonderful light. Once you were not a people, but now you are the people of God. 1 Peter ch.2 v5, v9-10

You are a holy priesthood. It is not elders nor deacons as ministers of the church, but you can pray to God the heavenly Father, he wants you to pray and worship him and come to face him.

If we confess our sins, he is faithful and just and will forgive us our sins and purify us from all unrighteousness. 1 John ch.1 v9 (see Matthew ch.6 v9-13).

There is no need for a priest, it was a Jewish practice. If you confess your sins, he will forgive your sins, regardless of the sin you offer to him.

The Points to Remember

The significant things to point out from all the churches would be:

- If you were a believer, you could go into any church regardless of the division that man has created or some rules or traditions.

- The apostles went around speaking to a church and there were not any suggestions that they were unpopular and unwelcome. They wrote down their letters in the New Testament.

- The church had several people that moved around from one church to another and they were invited to remain in that church. Each church was different from the others because they all had different believers and divergent races. But they were all one.

- Brothers wrote a letter of introduction there to welcome him to the disciples of the church (see Acts ch.18 v27).

- The head of every church was Jesus Christ. It should be the church of God. Where Jesus was in control not any man's thinking, reasoning or traditions.

"God has placed all things under his feet and appointed him to be head over everything for the church, which is his body, the fullness of him who fills everything in every way." Ephesians ch.1 v22-23

- We don't need priests; we can go to God as our Father in heaven.

For there is one God and one mediator between God and men, the man Christ Jesus. 1 Timothy ch.2 v5

- If the church is one, we respond to the Holy Spirit living in us. Otherwise, we must certainly fail. To avoid false teachers and prophets coming in to deceive the church, we must focus on what Jesus taught and not on human traditions or rules.

Those who live according to the sinful nature have their minds set on what that nature desires; but those who live in accordance with the Spirit have their minds set on what the Spirit desires. The mind of sinful man is death, the mind controlled by the Spirit is life and peace. Romans ch.8 v5-6

- The missionaries and others taught the gospel and treasured God's word and worked and laboured in the Old Testament. The New Testament was not written when the churches were established, it came much later. The Old and New Testament were compiled and are really the same thing.

- The books of the Bible were treasured and passed round the churches, eventually ending up as the New Testament. Athanasius, Bishop of Alexandria in his Easter letter of AD 367, gave a list of exactly the same books as the New Testament.

- There was no church that had everything. Apostles, teaching, prophecy and giving. This is why the believers moved around, helping the church to be formed and encouraging others to live lives that will follow Jesus.

- Most church were small and there was not any church building. They met in their homes or other places to be together and pray. The breaking of bread in their homes and certainly not in the church (see Acts ch.2 v46).

- If you want to go into a new church, there is no question to fill in, no assessment to complete, no survey to add to. If you are a believer, you can come in with full membership and be treated as if you were always there. All you have to do is by baptism (see Matthew ch.28 v19) by which the believers in the church will welcome you.

- If you want to be baptised, it can be done immediately, like in the river if you trust the Lord as your Saviour. Like the Ethiopian eunuch an important official in charge of the treasury of Candace queen of the Ethiopian. He was baptised on his route to go back home.

"Look, here is water. Why shouldn't I be baptised?" And he gave the orders to stop the chariot. Then both Philip and the eunuch went down into the water and Phillip baptised him. Acts ch.8 v37-38

- Baptism is an identity with Jesus, going down in to the water as he was crucified and died, coming up out of the water as Jesus was raised up from the dead. It indicates a new spirit, the past is gone and buried.

- The elders should be shepherding and caring for the flock. This is what Jesus mentioned after he was raised up form the dead. (see John ch.21 v15-17). It is important for us to understand what God has done and what we should do.

- There is no mention of any problems with the church, nothing to bar the church from meeting, even in Corinth. The elders had to manage the church under Jesus, to shepherd the believers with the word of the Lord.

- There was no outreach, when they had prayed they spoke the word fearlessly and confident that others would hear. Each person spoke the word boldly and went around in their place of home, school and work.

After they prayed, the place were they were meeting was shaken. And they were all filled with the Holy Spirit and spoke the word of God boldly. Acts ch.4 v31

- This is where the Holy Spirit called them for the task to go out as missionaries, one with prayer and fasting. This is what the Holy Spirit can do. We are fragmented each with it own church, nobody knows what the other churches can or even do, nobody knows what the missionaries are doing and nobody even cares for them. Each one has its own missionary group.

While they were worshipping the Lord and fasting, the Holy Spirit said, "Set apart for me Barnabas and Saul for the work to which I have called them." Acts ch.13 v2

- The reason is that love governs a respect for God is valid as your neighbour as yourself. This is the reason that the church is still there and is one. But separated into groups of churches, that is bad and it defeats the work of the church to go out and reach the lost.

Love the Lord You God with all your heart and with all your soul and with all your mind and with all your strength. The second is this: love your neighbour as yourself. There is no commandment greater than these. Mark ch.12 v30-31

- How can you tell if it is a believer? We all will have fruit whether it is good or bad. The good fruit will be those who do the will of God and trust in Jesus as God's only Saviour, the bad fruit will do the devil's work thereby pointing out the evil things they have done.

Jesus said, "A good tree cannot bear bad fruit, and a bad tree cannot bear good fruit. Every tree that does not bear good fruit is cut down and thrown into the fire. Thus, by their fruit you will recognise them" Matthew ch.7 v18-20

ONLY ONE CHURCH

We don't know how the church in one village, town or city can be like this? All getting together with one elders and deacons.

There is too much of all man's tradition will have to go, Anglican, Baptist, Brethren, Charismatic, Methodist, Roman Catholic, United Reform and many others. Plus, there are false prophets and false teachers in the church today, trying there best to spoil everything. Seeking what they thinking is best for believers to do. What about the church leaders, people who have gone to college to find out what they should be doing?

This is what Jesus Christ has in mind, he is very disappointed in what he sees. Everyone going to a church building totally separate from the others. Do you know all the names of the believers in your town? Or even the elders?

There are three instances of what is wrong with us:

- A separate building collapsed bringing down the front of the roof, fortunately no one was hurt but it was early in the day. We were told about it, because the current news would explain to everyone, but the building was old. But nobody went round there and helped them, they had to clear the remains up and repair it. It was not the same as our church, nobody asked them to come in and pray, or even help them to clear it up.

- On a beach mission we had a lot of people going there, all kinds of churches were there. One member of our church tried to get another member to fit in with what our church was doing. There was a lot of prayer and soul searching, but it was a hopeless mess, they failed to understand the difference. It was one solitary church doing the beach mission.

- We had a play outside our church each year and the town would have a party. We had tracts giving a gospel message, but unfortunately one person was not in our church and was speaking to people. The elders got together and said, "This is our play, why don't you move along on another street and speak to people there." He was basically moved on.

We don't really understand that the believers are all in one town, regardless of the views that they hold. The three instances, separate us from the rest of the believers and that will mean we lose out. The rest of the crowd didn't understand, they thought that it was a petty thing, the world didn't know that the Father sent the Son to die on the cross for all of us.

To let the world, know that you sent me and have loved them even as you have loved me. John ch.17 v23

If in a town that you recognise any believers, whether in or another church, we all will have a work to do. Sharing the gospel of the Lord, praying and worshipping the Lord. Coming together together, holding fast to what we believe, simply a creed:

I believe in God, the Father Almighty.

Creator of heaven and earth.

I believe in Jesus Christ, his only Son our Lord.

He was conceived by the power of the Holy Spirit.

He suffered, crucified, died and was finally buried.

On the third day he rose again.

He ascended into heaven and is seated with the Father.

He will come again to judge the living and the dead.

I believe in the Holy Spirit; he will convict the world.

With regard to sin, righteousness and judgement.

To take us to the kingdom of God.

It is only God that matters, Father, Son and Holy Spirit.

Qualifications for Believers

Certain themes reoccur when Paul instructed Timothy and Titus throughout his pastoral letters.   He said, 'When you have elders and deacons what should they be like?' I would suggest this is what the believers should be doing:

Outside Interests - away from others

    Does not pursue dishonest gain.

    Has a good reputation with outsiders.

    Not a lover of money.

    Not given to drunkenness.

    Not quarrelsome.

    Not quick tempered.

    Not overbearing.

    Not violent but gentle.

Inside Interests - in the church

    Able to teach.

    Hospitable.

    Husband of one wife.

    Keeps hold of the truth.

    Loves what is good.

Manages his own family well.

Not a recent convert.

Sees that his children obey him.

Well Meaning - both in and out of the church

Blameless.

Disciplined.

Respectable.

Self controlled.

Sincere.

Temperate.

Tested.

Upright and holy.

This is what the believer should be doing. This is what the Lord thinks that the elders should be shepherding for his sheep and lambs. Both inside and outside of his church and that means disciplining and protecting his believers.

CHURCH GOING FORWARD

I don't know what the one church will be like. But first, we must put aside all the man-made traditions and focus on what the Bible teaches. It is clearly put, only one Lord and master, Jesus Christ who leads and heads the church.

Secondly, if one truly studies the Bible there is only one church. We have the elders in each church to look after the believers. If the elders are not fit enough then the church will die. Several churches have lost their way and no longer appear among us.

The elders are very important to hold the church together.

Paul and Barnabas appointed elders for them in each church and, with prayer and fasting, committed them to Lord, in whom they had us their trust. Acts ch.14 v23

The work of the church should be to appoint elders.

That he can encourage others by sound doctrine and refute those who oppose it. Titus ch.1 v9

Avoid senseless matters because they take you away from Jesus Christ.

The elders who direct the affairs of the church well are worthy of double honour, especially those whose work is preaching and teaching. 1 Timothy ch.5 v17

The elders whose work in preaching and teaching are worth of double honour. Why? Because it is important that they instruct the church. All the elders were to exercise leadership.

This is what Jesus says:

My prayer is not that you (the Father) take them out of the world but that you protect them from the evil one John ch.17 v15

If the role of elders to protect the believers from the evil one who tries to influence them with false, teachers and prophets in the church. The elders were to especially work hard to instruct and study the scriptures regularly to make sure that all the teaching and prophesying comes from God above (see 1 John ch.4 v1-6).

This is the work of the church.